Great Joy

LifeThemes
S E R I E S

Great Joy

A 31-Day Devotional

J.I. PACKER
COMPILED BY
BETH NETHERY FEIA

ViB
VINE
BOOKS

SERVANT PUBLICATIONS
ANN ARBOR, MICHIGAN

Vine Books is an imprint of Servant Publications especially designed to serve evangelical Christians.

Scripture used in this work, unless otherwise indicated, is taken from the HOLY
BIBLE: NEW INTERNATIONAL VERSION (NIV) © 1973, 1978, 1984
International Bible Society. Used by permission of Zondervan Bible Publishers.
Excerpts from *Hot Tub Religion,* © 1987 by J.I. Packer, used by permission of
Tyndale House Publishers, Inc. All rights reserved. Excerpts from *God's Words* ©
1988 by J.I. Packer, used by permission of Baker Book House Company. Excerpts
from *Rediscovering Holiness,* © 1992 by J.I. Packer, used by permission of Servant
Publications. Excerpts from *Growing in Christ,* © 1994 by J.I. Packer, used by permission of Good News Publishers/Crossway Books, Wheaton, Illinois 60187.
"Evangelical Foundations of Spirituality," from *Gott Lieben Und Seine Gebote Halten,*
ed., Bockmeuhl, M. & K. Burkhardt (Geissen: Brunnen Verlag, 1991). Used by permission.

Published by Servant Publications
P.O. Box 8617
Ann Arbor, Michigan 48107

Cover photograph: © W. Morgan/Westlight

98 99 00 01 10 9 8 7 6 5 4 3 2 1

Printed in the United States of America
ISBN 1-56955-093-X

LIBRARY OF CONGRESS CATALOGING-IN-PUBLICATION DATA

Packer, J.I. (James Innell)
Great joy : a 31-day devotional / J.I. Packer ; compiled by Beth Nethery Feia.
    p.   cm.   — (LifeThemes series)
Includes bibliographical references.
ISBN 1-56955-093-X (alk. paper)
1. Spiritual life—Meditations.   2. Joy—Religious aspects—Christianity—
Meditations.   3. Devotional calendars.   I. Feia, Beth.   II. Title.   III. Series.
BV4501.2.P234   1998
242'.2—dc21   98-14298
                                                    CIP

Contents

Foreword

Joy is one of the great Christian words, for at least three reasons.

Reason one: *because rejoicing is one of the great Christian activities.* "Rejoice in the Lord always," said Paul (Phil 4:4), and we are not really very good Christians if we are not setting ourselves to do just that.

Reason two: *because joy is at the heart of the great hope Christians are heirs to.* "You will fill me with joy in your presence, with eternal pleasures at your right hand," said David (Ps 16:11). Jesus' parable looks forward to the day when he will say to his faithful servants, "Come and share your master's happiness!" (the Greek says *joy:* Mt 25:21, 23). Christian rejoicing is training and rehearsing for heaven, where joy with Jesus will be the unending agenda.

Reason three: *because joy does the heart great good.* "A cheerful heart is good medicine" (Prv 17:22). In the modern Western world, where the family is disintegrating, moral standards are dropping, the intolerable is increasingly tolerated, and self-seeking and exploitation are increasingly the rule, there is little to be cheerful about. The words of Shelley, proto-hippie of two centuries ago, "Rarely, rarely, comest thou, Spirit of Delight!" are so poignantly true today that one can hardly speak them without tears. But Christians have sources of joy that the world knows nothing about. The Christian life, though no joyride, is itself a joy road, leading through great joy here to greater joy hereafter. The kingdom of God, writes Paul, is a matter "of righteousness, peace and joy in the Holy Spirit" (Rom 14:17), and the joy is truly life-transforming.

Mapping and marking out God's joy way for his adopted children is the service that this month-long sequence of meditations and devotions seeks to render. Credit for it must go to Beth Feia, who got the idea and made the selections. She saw clearly that true spiritual joy is only known where the quest for personal holiness and the quiet acceptance of things going wrong have replaced the frantic search for permanent painlessness and pleasure, and she chose accordingly. Thank you, Beth; you are right on target.

Joy, in the full Christian sense of the word, is a supreme contentment, a supreme peace, a supreme concentration on the source of joy, and a supreme happiness at the way things are for one. The path to the personal practice of joy, which is what rejoicing means, is a secret that too few of us know, so let me try to set it out now, as an orienting preview of the ground over which our month of meditation will take us. The path consists of seven attitudes and activities, which need to be pursued together. The state of joy is their exalted and energizing end product. Here is the analysis.

First, the practice of joy means *lifting your eyes.* "I lift up my eyes to the hills—where does my help come from? My help comes from the Lord, the Maker of heaven and earth," of whom the beauty, grandeur, and solidity of the hills is an emblem and a reminder (Ps 121:1-2). Instead of looking down at the ground, as the despairing and depressed do, look God-ward, every day and many times a day. Look up in wonder at the Father who in love gave his Son to become your Redeemer through his atoning death, and who sent the Spirit to be your Renovator through a life-imparting new birth. "I thought on the gospel until I was full of joy," wrote a cancer sufferer. Look up in gratitude for the promises of Scripture, which tell you that your Savior-God will guard you, guide you, keep you, feed you, care for you, uphold you, forgive your daily shortcomings, free you from Satan's snares and bondages, and shepherd you through this world to the next, where you will see and enjoy him forever. This action, you will find, will lead you to joy.

Second, the practice of joy means *leaving things behind*. The things in question are attitudes of self-absorption and self-pity, feelings of being a victim and a loser, all deliberately cultivated habits of self-centeredness and sin, and any spirit of bitterness and resentment toward God for allowing the various harms and hurts ("losses and crosses," as the Puritans put it) that have marked your life thus far. These things obstruct joy as roadblocks obstruct highways; you need to renounce them and tell God you are sorry you ever slipped into them. This action also, you will find, will lead you to joy.

Third, the practice of joy means *looking ahead*. "Store up for yourselves treasures in heaven," says Jesus, "where moth and rust do not destroy, and where thieves do not break in and steal. For where your treasure is, there your heart will be also" (Mt 6:20-21). "Heart" here means one's deepest desire, determination, and delight, all blended with a single focus. Think ahead, and dwell constantly on the joyful future for which I charge you to invest— that is Jesus' meaning. As it is natural for children to look forward to the coming excitements of parties and holidays, so it is natural for Christians to look forward to the coming excitements of a life better than this one, in closer fellowship with Jesus than ever they experience at present, and to think of these things often as they seek to serve their Lord here. This action, too, you will find, will lead you to joy.

Fourth, the practice of joy means *loving your Lord*. Love affairs in this world are supposed to bring joy, though in experience it does not always work out that way; but Christianity is a special kind of love affair, in which the link between love and joy is solid. As real lovers love to tell their loved ones what it is about them that they particularly love, so real Christians love to tell the Father and the Son how they love the mercy, the faithfulness, the wisdom, the gentleness, and all the other glories of the divine character that the ways of grace reveal. And as real lovers love to show their love by doing all they can to please their beloved ones, so real Christians love to ask themselves, as they love to ask their Lord, what is the most and best they can do to show him that they truly love him. When the risen Jesus had asked Peter, "Do you love me?" and Peter had said he did, Jesus told him in effect to prove it by feeding his sheep and lambs; serving them would show that Peter's love for Jesus was a reality (see Jn 21:15-17). Action of this kind, demonstrating by what you do that your love for Jesus is more than mere words, is yet another avenue, you will find, that will lead you to joy.

Fifth, the practice of joy means *losing your inhibitions.* Some of us are so emotionally frozen that we never get close to anyone, and feel paralyzed with embarrassment when urged to loosen up. Inner restraints of this kind block out joy in our relationships both with other people (even our nearest and dearest) and with God. For most of us, step one in losing our inhibitions is to sing psalms and hymns to the Father, the Son, and the Spirit, loud and long, both in church and on our own. In every generation the liveliest Christians have been great singers before the Lord, even if their voices have not been the best, and this is definitely an example to follow. Such action is a further factor, you will find, that will lead you to joy.

Sixth, the practice of joy means *letting created things impact you.* This is God's world, and every flower, every tree, every clump of grass, every sight of sunshine and sunset, moon and stars, every item of natural beauty and every bit of moral beauty—in short, everything that has value of any kind—should stir and excite us by the range and power of God's goodness that it shows us. The praises of God in the Psalms express a great deal of this excitement. Self-centeredness, unrecognized and unacknowledged as it may be, often makes people insensitive to the impact of things around them, and such insensitivity can only dishonor God the Creator, quench the Holy Spirit by frustrating his influence, and prolong joyless gloom in our hearts. Learning this openness to God, and unlearning the preoccupations that keep us from it, are other actions, you will find, that will lead you to joy.

Seventh, the practice of joy means *loving your neighbor:* taking an interest in others, helping them, bearing with them and forgiving them if need be, and never treating them merely as conveniences and means to one's own ends. Practical commitment to the service of others, even when—perhaps, especially when—you are in pain and under strain yourself, is yet one more line of action, you will find, that will lead to joy.

Joy is a habit, formed by cultivating the seven habits listed above. Paul lists it as one aspect of the many-sided fruit of the Spirit in Christian lives (see Gal 5:22), and all these aspects, when you look at them, prove to be behavior patterns expressing a purpose of glorifying God and an attitude of goodwill toward others. Christian joy is a sharing in the joy of Jesus, who on the eve of his betrayal, and foreknowing the dreadfulness of what was to come, could still tell his disciples that he had explained to them their need to abide in him and obey the Father, "so that my joy may be in you and that your joy may be complete" (Jn 15:11). How we need this joy! How easily we miss it! How sadly we suffer when we are living without it! How hard it is to endure the daily realities of pain, grief, loss, abuse, neglect, insult, injustice, and all life's other ills in this fallen world, when one has not yet learned to rejoice in the Lord! To Christians who had "had to suffer grief in all kinds of trials" Peter was able to write: "Though you have not seen [Christ], you love him; and even though you do not see him now, you believe in him and are *filled with an inexpressible and glorious joy,* for you are receiving the goal of your faith, the salvation of your souls" (1 Pt 1:8-9; emphasis added). May the truths set forth for learning, and the hymns proposed for praying and singing, in the pages that follow help us all into more of that inexpressible, glorious joy than any of us have known yet.

J.I. Packer

11

The Truth About Holiness

1

Our Heart's Deepest Longing

What sort of behavior is natural to the child of God? A widespread but misleading line of teaching tells us that Christians have two natures: an old one and a new one. They must obey the latter while denying the former. Sometimes this is illustrated in terms of feeding one of your two dogs while starving the other. The misleading thing here is not the reminder that we are called to holiness and not to sin, but that the idea of "nature" is not being used as it is used both in life and in Scripture (see, for example, Rom 2:14; Eph 2:3). The point is that "nature" means the whole of what we are, and the whole of what we are is expressed in the various actions and reactions that make up our life. To envisage two "natures," two distinct sets of desires, neither of which masters me till I choose to let it, is unreal and bewildering, because it leaves out so much of what actually goes on inside me.

The clearer and more correct thing to say, as I hope we all see, is this: we were born sinners by nature, dominated and driven from the start—and most of the time unconsciously—by self-seeking, self-serving, self-deifying motives and cravings. Being united to Christ in new birth through the regenerating work of the Spirit has so changed our nature that our heart's deepest desire (the dominant passion that rules and drives us now) is a copy, faint but real, of the desire that drove our Lord Jesus. That was the desire to know, trust, love, obey, serve, delight, honor, glorify, and enjoy his heavenly Father—a multi-faceted, many-layered desire for God, and for more of him than has been enjoyed so far.

The focus of this desire in Jesus was upon the Father, whereas in Christians it is upon the Father and the Son together (and the latter especially). But the nature of the desire is the same. The natural way for Christians to live is to let this desire determine and control what they do, so that the fulfilling of the longing to seek, know, and love the Lord becomes the mainspring of their life.

To walk with Christ in the path of holy discipleship is the life for which the hearts of Christians truly long. From this follows the equally momentous truth that obeying the promptings of indwelling sin (the sin that still marauds in the systems of Christians though it no longer masters their hearts) is not what they really want to do at all, for sinning is totally unnatural to them.

Why then do we ever do it?—let alone make a habit of doing it, as notoriously we sometimes do? Partly, no doubt, because we fail to recognize sin for what it is, through ignorance of God's standards. Partly, too, because we yield to the nagging pull of temptation, giving way though we know that we should not and need not. But partly, too, because we let ourselves be deceived into supposing that to give way to this or that inordinate desire—for food, drink, pleasure, ease, gain, advancement, or whatever—is what we really want to do.

Again and again it appears that Christians are not sufficiently in touch with themselves. They do not know themselves well enough to realize that, because of the way in which their nature has been changed, their hearts are now set against all known sin. So they hang on to unspiritual and morally murky behavior patterns, and kid themselves that this adds to the joy of their lives. Encouraged by Satan, the grand master of delusion, they feel (feelings as such, of course, are mindless and blind) that to give up these things would be impossibly painful and impoverishing, so though they know they should, they do not. Instead, they settle for being substandard Christians, imagining they will be happier that way. Then they wonder why their whole life seems to them to have become flat and empty.

The truth is that they are behaving in a radically unnatural way, one that offers deep-level violence to their own changed nature. In doing what they think they like, they are actually doing what their renewed heart—if they would only let it speak—would tell them that it dislikes intensely, not only because it brings guilt and shame before God but, more fundamentally, because it is in itself repulsive to the regenerate mentality. The regenerate heart cannot love what it knows God hates. So these Christians are behaving unnaturally, occupying themselves in activities against which their own inner nature revolts. Such behavior is always bad medicine, producing sadness, tension, and discontent, if not worse.

There is a venerable Christian term for this condition: *backsliding*. The unnatural act of backsliding is always to be avoided, both because it provokes our holy heavenly Father to discipline and correct us in a punitive way (as is explained in Hebrews 12:5-10), and also because, at some stage and in some measure, bitterness and misery are its ultimate and inescapable fruit. We must realize that all sin has the nature of suicidal, self-impoverishing madness, in the Christian life no less than elsewhere. To see this, and accordingly to commit oneself to follow one's heart by running in the path of God's calling and commands as hard and fast as one can, is the directional basis of holiness. Since that is the most truly natural course for any Christian to follow, it holds out a hope of deep happiness, heart-happiness, here and now, that can never be attained otherwise.

Rediscovering Holiness, pp. 83–87

Object of my first desire,
Jesus, crucified for me;
All to happiness aspire,
Only to be found in thee.
Thee to praise, and thee to know,
Constitute my bliss below;
Thee to see, and thee to love,
Constitute my bliss above.

Whilst I feel thy love to me,
Every object teems with joy;
May I ever walk with thee,
For 'tis bliss without alloy.
Let me but thyself possess,
Total sum of happiness:
Perfect peace I then shall prove,
Heaven below and heaven above.

Augustus Toplady

2

"I Want to Be Like Jesus"

Personal holiness is an issue for every believer without exception. I am really expected to be so much like Jesus Christ that others will know at once and unmistakably that I am a Christian. Each of us must reckon on going to school with Jesus our Lord to learn how to practice holiness.

Holiness is basically a relationship to God, which God himself graciously imparts to us. It is a relationship established by our justification (God's once-for-all act of pardoning and accepting us): hereby he claims us, or rather reclaims us, as his own, through the saving mediation of our Lord Jesus Christ, and so sets us apart for himself. Holiness or sanctification in this sense is always, only, and entirely the free gift of God. It is one aspect of the newness of life that union with Christ effects.

Believers are positionally holy (separated by God for himself) from the word "go." Their obligation to practice moral and spiritual holiness on a day-to-day basis is derived from that fact. Our setting ourselves apart for God, in purposed separation from the world, the flesh, and the devil, is our proper response—our only proper response—to the knowledge that God has already claimed us by right of redemption. He gives us his Spirit as a pledge and foretaste of glory. "Do you not know that your body is a temple of the Holy Spirit, who is in you, whom you have received from God? You are not your own; you were bought at a price. Therefore honor God with your body" (1 Cor 6:19-20). "Do not grieve the Holy Spirit of God, with whom you were sealed for the day of redemption" (Eph 4:30).

Holiness of life is not precisely a human achievement,

however much it demands of human effort. It is a work of the Holy Spirit, who prompts and energizes the human effort as part of it. We do not sanctify ourselves. On the contrary, conscious recognition that apart from Christ we can do nothing (see Jn 15:5), and prayerful dependence on him to enable us to do each thing that we know we should do, is a *sine qua non* of the holy life. Self-reliance is not the way of holiness, but the negation of it. Self-confidence in the face of temptation and conflicting pressures is a sure guarantee that some sort of moral failure will follow.

Holiness involves the two related but distinct aspects of Christian existence that are nowadays labeled spirituality and ethics. Spirituality includes everything that has to do with implementing a Christian's fellowship with God—meditation; prayer; worship; self-discipline; use of the means of grace; exercising faith, hope, and love; maintaining purity, peace, and patience of heart; seeking and serving God in all one's relationships; and giving God glory and thanks. Ethics covers the delineating of God's standards, the determining of his revealed will, and the development and display of those character qualities that constitute God's image in us who were made to be his image-bearers.

Spirituality without ethics corrupts itself by becoming morally insensitive and antinomian, more concerned to realize God's presence than to keep his law. Ethics without spirituality corrupts itself by becoming mechanical, formalistic, proud, and unspiritual. It follows the Pharisees in settling for self-righteous role-play and forgetting that holiness requires a humble heart. Holiness is an arch that rests on spirituality and ethics as its two pillars, and crashes down the moment either pillar crumbles.

Further, holiness is the imitation of Christ in his virtues of love to God and humanity, trust in the Father's goodness, acceptance of his will, submission to his providence, and zeal for his honor and glory.

Carefully and prayerfully modeling our attitudes and responses after those of Jesus is part of what holiness means. "I want to be like Jesus in my heart," say the words of a classic spiritual, and true holiness always wants that.

Rediscovering Holiness, pp. 90–94

ॐ

O to be like thee! blessed Redeemer,

This is my constant longing and prayer;

Gladly I'll forfeit all of earth's treasures,

Jesus, thy perfect likeness to wear.

O to be like thee! O to be like thee,

Blessed Redeemer, pure as thou art!

Come in thy sweetness, come in thy fullness—

Stamp thine own image deep on my heart.

ॐ

THOMAS O. CHISHOLM

3

Our Neglected Priority

I am concerned about holiness because it seems to me that today's Church is very, very insensitive at this point. I put it to you that holiness is a neglected priority of the modern Church. It was a priority for the Lord Jesus; he prayed that the Father would sanctify his disciples by the truth. Is it a priority for the people of God today? As I look around, I see a neglect of holiness.

What has happened to produce this neglect? Two things at least have gone wrong. First, our godliness (so called) is excessively man-centered. It focuses on "my personal sanctification" rather than "the glory of God." The emphasis is all on self-fulfillment, happiness, being shielded from trouble, and being enabled to succeed. Success in relationships, success in one's sex life, success in everyday activities, has become the name of the game. Book after book has been written to guide us to success in these areas. But I do not see that our eyes are on the Lord and that our supreme concern, the thing that consumes us and makes us run, is the glory of God. This means that at the level of motive our man-centeredness is leading us to neglect the reality of sanctification.

Second, our sanctity lapses again and again into activism, so that activism almost becomes our religion. By activism I mean that self-reliant activity whereby the whole of our Christianity is a matter of running around and doing things for God—being busy, busy, busy for God. We admire the busiest Christians. We take it for granted that they are the best Christians. We admire the rush and bustle of endless Christian activity. Some of us are spiritually barren because we are too busy even to pray; I tell you, brothers and sisters, if you are too busy to pray, you really are too busy.

A nineteenth-century pastor, Robert Murray McCheyne, of Dundee, Scotland, once said: "My people's greatest need is ..." How would you have expected him to finish that sentence? Nowadays, I would suppose, a lot of pastors would say, "My people's greatest need is that I should have counseling skills or expository skills or other ministerial skills." McCheyne did not talk that language. "My people's greatest need," he said, "is *my personal holiness.*" Do we think in those terms? Is that our vision? I fear not. Therefore, I say, holiness seems to me to be a neglected priority in today's Church, and it distresses me.

I take it further. I put it to you that holiness is a fading glory in the evangelical world. I put it to you that generations ago people cared about holiness and sanctification in a way we do not, and at that point they were in advance of us and we are now grievously behind them.

I think of the seventeenth-century Puritans for whom holiness was the watchword of life. I think about John Wesley, who said on more than one occasion that God raised up the Methodist movement, not primarily for evangelism but to "spread scriptural holiness throughout the land." I do not agree with Wesley's understanding of Christian holiness at every point. But I can only applaud him for putting holiness first and making it top priority in the spiritual movement that he sought to encourage.

Holiness, I repeat, is a fading glory in the evangelical world. We are preoccupied with controversy, scholarship, liberty in ethical matters, and we are disillusioned, I think, with the holiness teaching on which we were brought up. And perhaps that is not too wrong a reaction. There has been a type of holiness teaching that has been sterile and inadequate. Yet I was a little bothered (as well as amused) at what an inner-city pastor said to me in 1979. Somebody had asked, "What do you think of the victorious Christian life?" He replied, "It's all right if you've got the time and the money for it." You can see why I was amused. But can you see why I was bothered? Should Christians be able simply to shrug off the quest for holiness, as if it were a matter of secondary importance? According to the New Testament, at the very heart of our Christian living should be a passion in all things to obey God, imitate our Savior, resist sin, and please our gracious Father. Nothing can alter that priority.

"Predestination and Sanctification"
in *Tenth*, a periodical published by
Tenth Presbyterian Church, Philadelphia

৵

Take time to be holy, the world rushes on;
Much time spend in secret with Jesus alone;
By looking to Jesus, like him thou shalt be;
Thy friends in thy conduct his likeness shall see.

Take time to be holy, be calm in thy soul;
Each thought and each motive beneath his control;
Thus led by his Spirit to fountains of love,
Thou soon shalt be fitted for service above.

৵

WILLIAM D. LONGSTAFF

4

God's Gift and Your Task

The work of God could be compared to renovating a building while it continues in use. The building is you and I living our lives. In those lives of ours God is at work demolishing bad habits, the ways of the old man, and building up good, new habits of Christlike action and reaction. God is making us new.

In Philippians 2, Paul says, "Work out your salvation with fear and trembling, for it is God who works in you to will and to act according to his good purpose" (vv. 12, 13). God is doing something entirely supernatural in our lives. He is changing us into the image of the Lord Jesus. This cannot be explained in natural terms. It is the work of grace and of his indwelling Holy Spirit.

This is sanctification viewed from the divine angle, and we do well to have awe and reverence for it (which is what "fear and trembling" really means) and never to forget that our lives, characters, and innermost beings are the subject of a mysterious, transforming work of God. We should look for it in the lives of our brothers and sisters in Christ and rejoice when we see it. We should have very sensitive consciences concerning the work of God in our own lives lest we mar it by disobedience or sinful habits indulged.

But that is only half the story. The other angle on sanctification that the New Testament gives us is to show it as *the quality of a Christian's life*. From this standpoint the words that are used as close synonyms for sanctification are "righteousness" and "holiness." From this standpoint what we are talking about is obedience to God, the effort and disciplined activity of doing his will. This is what I call the "resistance movement" in the Christian life.

You know about the resistance movement in France, Holland, and other countries during the Second World War, in which German-occupying forces were resisted from the inside by loyal people. Well, in the Christian life there must also be a resistance movement: resistance to the allurements of the world, the flesh, and the devil, and to the power of bad habits still unbroken. There must be resistance to those seductions into wrong ways that are presented to us every day. "Live by the Spirit," says Paul, "and you will not gratify the desires of the sinful nature" (Greek, *flesh:* Gal 5:16).

From another standpoint sanctification involves the imitation of Christ—imitation, in fact, of both the Father and the Son in the love they have shown us. "Be imitators of God ... as dearly loved children," says the apostle Paul. "And live a life of love, just as Christ loved us and gave himself up for us, as a fragrant offering and sacrifice to God" (Eph 5:1, 2). We are to love because he first loved us. This is the discipline of imitating our Lord.

The human side of sanctification also involves the discipline of pleasing God. First Thessalonians 4:1 states it: "Finally, brothers, we instructed you how to live in order to please God, as in fact you are living."

Sanctification is a life, then, of obedience, of resisting sin, of imitating Jesus, and of fellowship with God as one seeks to please one's heavenly Father in everything one does. Are we living that sort of life? We ought to ask ourselves that right now, because this is what the real Christian life is all about—obeying the commands, resisting sin, imitating Christ, and pleasing the Father. These parameters of piety never change.

Sanctification, we now see, is both a gift (that is one side: God working in us to renew and transform us) and a task (the task of obedience, righteousness, and pleasing God). And we must never so stress either of the two sides that we lose sight of the other. Think only of the task, and you will become a self-reliant legalist seeking to achieve righteousness in your own strength. You will not make any headway at all. Think only of the work of God in your life, and the chances are that Satan will trick you into not making the necessary effort and not maintaining the discipline of righteousness so that, in fact, even as you rejoice in the work of God in your life you will be dishonoring it by your slackness. Hold both sides of the matter together in your mind, if you want your living to be right.

"Predestination and Sanctification"
in *Tenth*, a periodical published by
Tenth Presbyterian Church, Philadelphia

Oh, for a heart to praise my God,
A heart from sin free,
A heart that always feels the blood
So freely shed for me,

A heart resigned, submissive, meek,
My dear Redeemer's throne,
Where only Christ is heard to speak,
Where Jesus reigns alone,

A heart in every thought renewed,
Full of love divine,
Perfect and right and pure and good,
A copy, Lord, of thine.

CHARLES WESLEY

- 5 -

The New You

The New Testament speaks emphatically of the "newness" of the Christian's life in Christ, as compared and contrasted with all that went before. John, Peter, and James present the start of this newness as a new birth, and Paul presents it as a new creation, as co-resurrection with Jesus, and as putting off the old man and putting on the new man (see Eph 4:22; Col 3:9-10).

Putting off and putting on is the language of changing clothes, and when the NIV renders "man" as "self" it misses some of the meaning; what the Christian has put off is solidarity with Adam, and what he puts on is Christ, or solidarity with Christ, as the source and principle of his new life (cf. Rom 13:14; Gal 3:28).

Each image entails the thought of a totally fresh beginning: one has ceased to be what one was, and has commenced to be what previously one was not. Paul then charts the course of this newness in terms of being restored as God's image (see Col 3:10), serving righteousness and God as bondslaves of both (see Rom 6:16-23), and bringing forth the fruit of the Spirit (see Gal 5:22-25); John speaks of walking in the light (see 1 John 1:7); and indeed the whole body of New Testament writers labor the thought that Christians are called to live in a radically different way from those around them, and from the way they themselves lived before. The proclamation of newness as both a divine gift and a Christian obligation is loud and clear.

The theological and psychological reality of this great change is proclaimed in the dying-and-rising symbolism of baptism (cf. Rom 6:3f.; Col 2:12). The Holy Spirit unites us to the risen Christ. Intellectually the change is an opening and enlightening of the blinded mind to discern what previously we could not discern (see 2 Cor 4:3-6; Eph 1:17f.; cf. Lk 24:25, 31, 45)—namely, the spiritual realities of Christ and his salvation.

Motivationally, with the heart, the change is an implanting in us of the inclinations of Christ's perfect humanity through our ingrafting into him: this produces in us a mind-set and lifestyle that is not explicable in terms of what we were before. The Spirit-born person, as Jesus indicated, cannot but be a mystery to those who are not born again themselves; they can form no idea of what makes him tick (cf. Jn 3:8).

The New Testament enables us to form some idea of the characteristic exercise of heart that marks those whom God has thus brought into newness of life. Knowing the truth of the gospel, each will adore Christ as, in Newton's words,

> Jesus, my Shepherd, Husband, Friend,
> My Prophet, Priest, and King,
> My Lord, my Life, my Way, my End.

Seeing themselves as travelers on the way home, they will live by hope—hope, quite specifically, of meeting their beloved Savior face-to-face, and being with him forever. Discerning sinful desires in themselves despite their longing to be sin-free, and finding that in their quest for total righteousness their reach exceeds their grasp, they will live in tension and distress at their frustrating infirmities (cf. Rom 7:14-25). They will call on God as their heavenly Father, glorify and love him, honor and love other people, hate and fight evil in all its forms, grow downward into a deeper and more childlike humility, and practice patience under pressure. All this will at the same time go with determined obedience to God's law, conscious imitation of

Christ in attitude and purpose, and satisfying fulfillment of their own new instincts—in other words, naturalness in expressing their own new selves.

"Evangelical Foundations for Spirituality"
from *Gott Lieben Und Seine Gebote Halten*

~

Jesus, my all in all thou art;
My rest in toil, my ease in pain,
The medicine of my broken heart,
In war my peace, in loss my gain,
My smile beneath the tyrant's frown,
In shame my glory and my crown:
In want my plentiful supply,
In weakness my almighty power,
In bonds my perfect liberty,
My light in Satan's darkest hour,
In grief my joy unspeakable,
My life in death, my heaven in hell.

~

CHARLES WESLEY

Go and Sin No More

6

Turning Away From Sin

What is repentance? What does it mean to repent?

The term is a personal and relational one. It signifies going back on what one was doing before, and renouncing the misbehavior by which one's life in the world or one's relationship with God was being harmed. In the Bible, repentance is a theological term, pointing to an abandonment of those courses of action in which one defied God by embracing what he dislikes and forbids. The Hebrew word for repenting signifies turning, or returning. The corresponding Greek word carries the sense of changing one's mind so that one changes one's ways too. Repentance means altering one's habits of thought, one's attitudes, outlook, policy, direction, and behavior, just as fully as is needed to get one's life out of the wrong shape and into the right one. Repentance is in truth a spiritual revolution. This, now, and nothing less than this, is the human reality that we are to explore.

Repenting in the full sense of the word—actually changing in the way described—is only possible for Christians, believers who have been set free from sin's dominion and made alive to God. Repenting in this sense is a fruit of faith, and as such a gift of God (cf. Acts 11:18). The process can be alliteratively analyzed under the following headings:

1) Realistic recognition that one has disobeyed and failed God, doing wrong instead of doing right. This sounds easier than it actually is. T.S. Eliot spoke the truth when he observed: "Humankind cannot bear very much reality." There is nothing like a shadowy sense of guilt in the heart to make us passionately play the game of pretending something never happened, or rationalizing to ourselves action that was morally flawed. So, after David had committed adultery with Bathsheba and compounded it with murder, he evidently told himself that it was simply a matter of royal prerogative and, therefore, nothing to do with his spiritual life. So he put it out of his mind, until Nathan's "You are the man!" (2 Sm 12:7) made him realize, at last, that he had offended God. This awareness was, and is, the seedbed where repentance grows. It does not grow elsewhere. True repentance only begins when one passes out of what the Bible sees as *self-deception* (cf. Jas 1:22, 26; 1 Jn 1:8) and modern counselors call *denial,* into what the Bible calls *conviction of sin* (cf. Jn 16:8).

2) Regretful remorse at the dishonor one has done to the God one is learning to love and wanting to serve. This is the mark of the contrite heart (cf. Ps 51:17; Is 57:15). The Middle Ages drew a useful distinction between *attrition* and *contrition* (regret for sin prompted by fear for oneself and by love for God, respectively; the latter leads to true repentance while the former fails to do so). The believer feels, not just attrition, but contrition, as did David (see Ps 51:1-4, 15-17). Contrite remorse, springing from the sense of having outraged God's goodness and love, is pictured and modeled in Jesus' story of the prodigal's return to his father (see Lk 15:17-20).

3) Reverent requesting of God's pardon, cleansing of conscience, and help to not lapse in the same way again. A classic example of such requesting appears in David's prayer of penitence (see Ps 51:7-12). The repentance of believers always, and necessarily, includes the exercise of faith in God for these restorative blessings. Jesus himself teaches God's children to pray "forgive us our sins ... and lead us not into temptation" (Lk 11:4).

4) Resolute renunciation of the sins in question, with deliberate thought as to how to keep clear of them and live right for the future. When John the Baptist told Israel's official religious elite "Produce fruit in keeping with repentance" (Mt 3:8), he was calling on them to change direction in this way.

5) Requisite restitution to any who have suffered material loss through one's wrongdoing. Restitution in these circumstances was required by the Old Testament law. When Zacchaeus, the renegade Jewish taxman, became Jesus' disciple, he committed himself to make fourfold retribution for each act of extortion, apparently on the model of Moses' requirement of four sheep for every one stolen and disposed of (see Ex 22:1; cf. Ex 22:2-14; Lv 6:4; Nm 5:7).

An alternative alliteration (as if one were not enough!) would be:

1. *discerning* the perversity, folly, and guilt of what one has done;
2. *desiring* to find forgiveness, abandon the sin, and live a God-pleasing life from now on;
3. *deciding* to ask for forgiveness and power to change;
4. *dealing* with God accordingly;
5. *demonstrating,* whether by testimony and confession, by changed behavior, or by both together, that one has left one's sin behind.

Such is the repentance—not just the initial repentance of the adult convert, but the recurring repentance of the adult disciple—that is our present theme.

Rediscovering Holiness, pp. 122–25

❧

I've wandered far away from God—
Now I'm coming home;
The paths of sin too long I've trod—
Lord, I'm coming home.

I've wasted many precious years—
Now I'm coming home;
I now repent with bitter tears—
Lord, I'm coming home.

I've tired of sin and straying, Lord—
Now I'm coming home;
I'll trust thy love, believe thy word—
Lord, I'm coming home.

My soul is sick, my heart is sore—
Now I'm coming home;
My strength renew, my hope restore—
Lord, I'm coming home.

❧

WILLIAM J. KIRKPATRICK

7

Why Continual Repentance?

God is the Creator, who brought everything into being for his own pleasure, and on whom everything depends for its existence every moment. He has a right to prescribe how his rational creatures should behave. He has done this in his moral law, which requires us to be holy as he is holy—like him on our own human level in our character and our conduct, in our desires, our decisions, and our delights. We are required in all circumstances to be honest, godly, single-minded, energetic, passionate persons who behave at all times in a Jesus-like way, with hearts aflame, heads cool, and all our wits about us. Total righteousness is called for, expressing total devotion and commitment. We are assured that nothing less will do.

The purity and uprightness of God's own character, and his judgments of value (what is good and worthwhile, and what is neither) are fixed and immutable. He cannot be other than hostile to individuals and communities that flout his law. He cannot do other than visit them sooner or later in displays of retributive judgment, so that all his rational creatures may see the glory of his moral inflexibility.

Because of God's majesty as sovereign ruler of the universe, sin (lawlessness, missing the moral mark, failing to practice righteousness with all one's heart and soul) is a major matter. Secular Western culture, which has deliberately atrophied the sense of God's majesty, finds this hard to believe, but it is so. Some sins are intrinsically greater and intrinsically worse than others—but there can be no small sins against a great God.

God's purpose in our creation, as in our new creation, is that we should be holy. Therefore, moral casualness and unconcern as to whether or not we please God is in itself supremely evil. No expressions of creativity, heroism, or nice-guy behavior can cancel God's displeasure at being disregarded in this way.

God searches our hearts as well as weighs our actions. For this reason, guilt for sin extends to deficiencies in our motives and our purposes, as well as in our performance. T.S. Eliot wrote of "the greatest treason: To do the right deed for the wrong reason," and God observes and assesses our reasons for action as thoroughly as he does the actions themselves. In one sense, indeed, it is true to say that God focuses more attention on the heart—the thinking, reacting, desiring, decision-making core and center of our being—than he does on the deeds done, for it is by what goes on in our hearts that we are most truly known to him.

God is good and gracious to all his creatures, and has so loved the world as to give his only Son to suffer on the cross for our salvation. Active thanksgiving that expresses thankfulness of heart is the only proper response, and is in fact one of God's permanent requirements. Unthankfulness and unlove toward himself are as culpable in his sight as are any forms of untruthfulness and unrighteousness in dealing with our fellow humans. Transgressing the first and greatest commandment has to be the first and greatest sin (see Mt 22:34-40).

God promises to pardon and restore all who repent of their sin. Because sin, both of omission and commission, in motive, aim, thought, desire, wish, and fantasy even if not in outward action, is a daily event in Christians' lives (you know this about yourself, don't you?), regular repentance is an abiding necessity. Repentance must be thorough, coming from the heart just as did the sin. Repentance expresses in a direct way the regenerate heart's desire to cleave to God, and to love and please him constantly. It is this desire that begets the purpose of forsaking the sin and returning contritely to the Lord.

Regenerate persons know that sin when cherished becomes an obstacle to their enjoyment of fellowship with God. It prompts God to withdraw their assurance and make them feel his displeasure through inward as well as outward chastening. Therefore, their instinct is constantly to pray with the psalmist: "Search me, O God, and know my heart; test me and know my anxious thoughts. See if there is any offensive way in me, and lead me in the way everlasting" (Ps 139:23).

Rediscovering Holiness, pp. 134–37

Search me, O God, my actions try,
And let my life appear
As seen by thine all-searching eye;
To mine my ways make clear.

Search all my sense and know my heart,
Who only canst make known,
And let the deep, the hidden part
To me be fully shown.

Throw light into the darkened cells
Where passion reigns within;
Quicken my conscience till it feels
The loathsomeness of sin.

Search all my thoughts, the secret springs,
The motives that control,
The chambers where polluted things
Hold empire o'er the soul.

FRANCIS BOTTOME

8

Learn to Hate Sin

The God whom we claim to love and serve delights in righteousness and hates sin. Scripture is very clear about that. "Your eyes are too pure to look on evil; you cannot tolerate wrong" (Hab 1:13; see also Ps 5:4; Prv 6:16-19; 11:20; 12:22).

Those who neglect the discipline of thorough repentance for their shortcomings, along with regular self-examination so as to discern those shortcomings, are behaving as if God just turns a blind eye to our moral flaws—which is actually to insult him, since such indifference would be a moral flaw in itself. But God is not morally indifferent, and we must not act toward him as if he were. The truth is that the only way to show real respect for God's real purity is by realistically setting oneself against sin. That means not only a wholehearted purpose of pleasing God by consecrated zeal in keeping his law, it also means repentance. And repentance means not mere routine words of regret as one asks for pardon without one's heart being involved, but a deliberate confessing, an explicit self-humbling, and a sensing of shame in the presence of God as one contemplates one's failures. For God's purity, as we have seen, leads him to hate evil. His demand that we be like him requires us to become haters of it too, starting with the evil that we find inside ourselves.

It will help us here to look at a classic Bible passage that profiles repentance from the inside. In Psalm 51, according to tradition, David goes public by poeticizing the penitence he expressed to God after being convinced of his sin in the matter of Bathsheba and Uriah. He broke the tenth commandment by coveting his neighbor's wife, the eighth by stealing her, the seventh by committing adultery with her, the ninth indirectly, by trying to fool Uriah so that he would treat the coming child as his own, and the sixth directly, by liquidating Uriah at long range. Then David spent a year shrugging off what he had done until Nathan, acting as God's spokesman, showed him God's displeasure at it (see 2 Sm 11–12). But in Psalm 51 we meet a David who has come to his senses, and is now expressing repentance very fully, in six distinct stages, thus:

1) Verses 1-2 are *a plea for mercy and forgiveness.* They show a true understanding of God's covenant. The covenant whereby God and human beings commit themselves to belong to each other forever is the basis of all biblical religion. When God's servants stumble and fall, God's faithfulness to the covenant to which they have been unfaithful is their only hope. This covenant relationship is emphatically a gift of grace on God's part. It is he who initiates and sustains it, enduring all the follies and vices of his covenant partners. For God's holy ones were, are, and remain silly, sinful creatures, who can live before him only through being continually forgiven for their constant shortcomings. To this forgiveness, however, repentance is the only road.

2) Verses 3-6 are *an acknowledgment of guilt and the punishment we deserve for our sins.* They show understanding of sin, as our inbred perversity of heart that finds its expression in sins, specific acts of evil and wrongdoing in God's sight. The deep truths here are: first, we are not sinners because we sin, but rather we sin because we are sinners (vv. 5-6); second, all our sins, our inhumanities no less than our idolatries, are sins against God (v. 4).

3) Verses 7-9 are *a heart-cry for cleansing from sin and cancelation of guilt.* They show understanding of salvation as a work of

God restoring joy in fellowship with himself through the assurance of sins forgiven. David's "bones" (his conscious self, the person he knows himself to be) are "crushed" (rendered unable to function properly) as a result of his condemning conscience. He asks that his "bones" may be made literally to "dance" (as all the translations say, "rejoice") by the bestowing of this assurance (v.8)—a vivid metaphor for the revitalizing of one's inner life that knowledge of one's forgiveness brings.

4) Verses 10-12 are *a petition for quickening and renewing in God*. They show an understanding of spiritual life as essentially the steady, positive response of the human spirit to God—a response that is called forth and kept in being by the regenerative ministry of the indwelling Spirit of God himself. It is God's way to remove our demerit, our defilement, and our deviancy together. He does not save us in our sins, but from our sins. Whom he justifies he also sanctifies. Where there is no sign of a pure heart (a sin-hating heart that reflects the purity of God) or of a "steadfast ... willing" spirit (a disposition to honor and obey God and resist temptations to sin), we may well doubt whether the person is in a state of grace in any sense at all.

5) Verses 13-17 are *a promise to proclaim God's pardoning mercy in witness and in worship*. The verses show an understanding of ministry to both God and our fellow beings: to the holy God, by thankful praise; and to sinful humans, by proclaiming to them the grace that saves. Saints, let us note, are saved to serve—to celebrate and share what God has given them. Fresh dedication to doing this, in addition to all other good works, is one token of reality in repentance.

6) Verses 18-19 are *a prayer for the blessing of the Church,* God's Jerusalem, the people on earth who bear his name. The verses show an understanding of what most delights God—saved sin-

ners, penitents who are now pardoned and prospering spiritually, being moved by gratitude and joy to offer "righteous sacrifices" (v.19). (The thought here is of love-gifts to God, though the slaughtered bullocks of which David speaks might not immediately suggest that to the modern mind.) David's intercession for all God's people is not really a change of theme from the penitence that he was expressing before. Intercession springs naturally from the experiences of God's pardoning love that repentance triggers. Knowledge that one is loved will call forth love for others, and love for others will lead us to pray for them.

David honored the purity of God by the way he repented of his shameful misdeeds. Humbling himself, he acknowledged the provocation he had given, sought deliverance from the power as well as the guilt of his sins, and pledged himself afresh to do God's work and advance his praise. This was true repentance, and as such is a model for us.

Rediscovering Holiness, pp. 144–49

‿❧

Return, O holy Dove, return,
Sweet messenger of rest;
I hate the sins that made thee mourn
And drove thee from my breast.

The dearest idol I have known,
Whate'er that idol be,
Help me to tear it from thy throne
And worship only thee.

So shall my walk be close with God,
Calm and serene my frame;
So purer light shall mark the road
That leads me to the Lamb.

‿❧

WILLIAM COWPER

9

Holy Discontent

Clearer perceptions of God's purity have a reflex effect, as if that purity were a light shining into the recesses of the self and showing up all that had been lurking in the dark there. The things revealed include:

- stubborn habits of sin;
- chronic patterns of moral evasion;
- weaknesses of moral character;
- cravings that are really vicious;
- attitudes that are really arrogant;
- behavioral flaws due to temperament;
- inclinations to self-aggrandizement, self-indulgence, and self-pity;
- built-in self-protectiveness because of past hurts;
- moral quirks due to scars of abuse and layers of fear.

All of these faults and many more like them are now thrown into relief, as it were. One has to face them. The meaning of moral perfection—perfect love, humility, joy, peace, goodness, patience, gentleness, wisdom, fidelity, reliability, courage, fair-mindedness, and so on—is etched on the mind more clearly. The distance between that perfection and our own performance, looked at from the standpoint both of motivation and of execution, is perceived willy-nilly. Personal limitations for which we once made excuses to ourselves now seem indefensible. We wince, maybe even weep, at our own former crassness on moral matters.

Like Isaiah in the temple, so with Christians everywhere. The more vividly they see how holy God is, the more poignantly they feel how sinful and corrupt they are themselves. Because spiritual advance thus enlarges insight into the depths of one's own fallenness, those going forward in holiness often feel they are going backward. Their deepened awareness of how sinful they still are, despite their longing to serve God flawlessly, weights them down. As we have seen already, it calls forth from them their own "wretched man" heart-cry, echoing Paul's in Romans 7:24. Over and over again they dare to hope that they have overcome the downdrag of sin in some area of life. Over and over again God humbles them by letting them discover that it is not yet so. Though knowledge of gospel grace brings them joys in abundance, they are from this standpoint distressed.

This does not, however, mean that they are in an unhealthy spiritual state. Paul's own "wretched man" outburst is the word of the dynamic, spiritually healthy man who is dictating the letter to the Romans. His argument has led him to review what the law tells him about himself as he walks the path of new life in Christ (see Rom 6:1-14; 7:4-6; 8:1-39). From the fact that he could not feel healthy, or claim to be healthy, as he groaned under the burden of not yet being morally perfect as he wanted to be (see Rom 7:22; 8:23), some have inferred that either he really was not healthy or that in Romans 7:14-25 he was not writing about himself at all, despite his use of "I" and the present tense. They have taken for granted that no spiritually healthy person could feel about himself the way Paul does. But this is not so.

Intense distress at one's continuing imperfection, in the context of an intense love of goodness as God defines it and an intense zeal to practice it, is the clearest possible sign of the holiness of heart that is central to spiritual health. The paradox— too hard a nut, it seems, for some to crack—is that increase of real holiness always brings increase of real discontent, because of what has not yet been achieved. The truth is that the sense of frustrated longing that the "wretched man" heart-cry expresses belongs to the experience of all those who seek to live joyfully in the power of the Spirit and so please their Savior-God.

Rediscovering Holiness, pp. 220–23

ॐ

O Jesus Christ, grow thou in me,
And all things else recede;
My heart be daily nearer thee,
From sin be daily freed.

Each day let thy supporting might
My weakness still embrace;
My darkness vanish in thy light,
Thy life my death efface.

Make this poor self grow less and less,
Be thou my life and aim;
O make me daily, through thy grace,
More meet to bear thy name.

ॐ

J.C. LAVATER

10

Draining the Life Out of Sin

The Christian is committed to a lifelong fight against the world, the flesh, and the devil. Mortification is his assault on the second. Two texts from Paul show that it is an essential ingredient in Christian living: "Mortify therefore your members which are upon the earth" (Col 3:5, KJV; "Put to death, therefore, whatever belongs to your earthly nature," NIV); "If by the Spirit ye mortify the deeds of the body, ye shall live" (Rom 8:13, KJV; "Put to death the misdeeds of the body," NIV).

Christian privilege makes mortification obligatory. Paul argues thus (Col 3:1-5): "As those who now share Christ's risen life, whose citizenship and prospects are in the heavenly realm, who are no more children of wrath but sons of God and heirs of glory, you must behave as befits your status. You must be what you are, and not what you were. Therefore you must mortify sin." The second tells us that mortification is necessary as a means to an end. It is the way to "life," spiritual well-being in this world and glory with Christ in the next. It will not earn us life (Christ has done that for us already), but it is part of the work of faith (see 1 Thes 1:3) through which we lay hold and keep hold of Christ's free gift (cf. 1 Tm 6:12; Phil 3:12-14). It is one of the "works" without which "faith" (i.e., a profession of faith) is "dead" (see Jas 2:26). Paul's argument may be expanded thus: if you would make your calling and election sure by proving your faith true, if you would so run as to obtain, so travel as to arrive, you must mortify sin. "He who doth not kill sin in his way," observed the Puritan theologian John Owen, grimly, "takes no steps towards his journey's end."

The evident importance of the subject makes the long-standing neglect of it among Christians appear both sad and odd. One cause is surely the shallowness of Christian understanding and experience in these days. Since we hardly know God and so hardly know ourselves, and since most of us think of self-examination as old-fashioned and morbid, and never try it, we are hardly aware of indwelling sin at all.

There is an old comedy short (maybe one of Mack Sennett's, I can't be sure) in which an escaped lion takes the place of the shaggy dog beside the armchair and the comic affectionately runs his fingers through its mane several times before realizing that, as we say, he has a problem. We act like that with regard to our sinful habits. We treat them as friends rather than killers, and never suspect how indwelling sin when indulged enervates and deadens. This, one fears, is because we are already its victims, never having known what it is to be really alive in our relationship with God, just as children born with crippled legs never know what it is to run around, as distinct from hobbling. Such is the nemesis of our modern neglect of mortification.

Mortification is war; and four steps are involved in effective warfare. Two I will describe in this meditation, and two I will describe in the following meditation.

Step 1: We must know our enemy. The starting point in mortification is recognizing that we fight, not merely sins, but *sin*. The Bible portrays sin as a hereditary impulse, rooted deep in our nature, which drives us continually into a blind opposition toward God. Sin is a lust for self-assertion in defiance of God; the very idea of conscious dependence, grateful worship, and obedient fellowship with the Creator is utterly abhorrent to it. It is the root of all actual sins, and so of fallen man's family likeness to the devil.

Sin enslaves the unbeliever completely (cf. Rom 6:16-23). He is at peace with it, for it has won his heart. But the convert takes Christ as his master and model, and resolves that he will no longer be the self-asserting, God-resisting person he was. This is his "change of mind" (which is what *metanoia*, the Greek word for "repentance," really means). He renounces sin; he wills it death in him; and thus in intention he has "crucified the sinful nature" and its lusts (see Gal 5:24).

But sin does not forthwith die. On the contrary, it takes on a life of its own, and the Christian now finds it active within him as a kind of devilish alter ego, a shadow-self, opposing, resisting, and to a greater or lesser degree thwarting all his attempts to do the will of God.

The Christian thus finds himself in conflict with a part of himself: "the desires of the flesh are against the Spirit, and the desires of the Spirit are against the flesh ... to prevent you from doing what you would" (Gal 5:17). He wants to be perfect, but he never is, and at every stage of his life he is forced to say with Paul: "the good which I would I do not; but the evil which I would not, that I practice ... it is no more I that do it, but sin which dwelleth in me" (Rom 7:19-20, RV). Sin is already at war with us (see Rom 7:23; 1 Pt 2:11). It seeks our ruin; and the only way to preserve ourselves is to fight back. This we do by mortification.

Step 2: We must know our objective. In ignorance of one's enemy, one fights blind; without a clear objective, one fights aimlessly, "as one beating the air." We must, then, be clear as to what we are trying to do.

The two words translated "mortify" in the texts with which we began this study both mean "put to death," which is how most modern versions render them. This, then, is our aim: so to drain the life out of sin that it never moves again. We are not promised that we shall reach our goal in this life, but we are commanded to advance toward it by assaulting those inclinations and habits in which sin's presence is recognized. We are not merely to resist its attacks. We are to take the initiative against it. We must seek not merely the *counteraction,* but the *eradication* of it. Killing, so far as we can compass that, is the end in view.

Mortification is *a life's work.* Sin "will not otherwise die, but by being gradually and constantly weakened," warns Owen; "spare it, and it heals its wounds, and recovers strength." The Bible and Church history bear repeated witness to the disastrous consequences of ceasing to mortify before sin is dead. And it never dies in this world, however weak it may grow.

Moreover, mortification is *a painful discipline.* Sinful habits have become so much part of ourselves that to attempt their destruction is like cutting off a hand, or plucking out an eye (see Mt 5:29-30). "Carnal self," which, naturally enough, longs to live, will do all it can to deter us from the task of killing it.

Nonetheless, mortification is *an effective discipline.* It is part of healthy Christian experience to enjoy a continually increasing degree of deliverance from sins, as by mortification the strength of sin is steadily drained. And few things afford the Christian such relief and encouragement as the memory of sins that once ruled him, but that he has conquered by the power of the Spirit of God.

God's Words, pp. 181–85

꙰

I want a sober mind,
A self-renouncing will,
That tramples down, and casts behind
The baits of pleasing ill;
A soul inured to pain,
To hardship, grief, and loss;
Bold to take up, firm to sustain,
The consecrated cross.

I want a godly fear,
A quick discerning eye,
That looks to thee when sin is near,
And sees the tempter fly;
A spirit still prepared,
And armed with jealous care;
For ever standing on its guard,
And watching unto prayer.

꙰

CHARLES WESLEY

11

Fighting and Winning the Battle

Step 3: We must know our superiority. Nobody has much heart for a fight he does not think he can win. To expect defeat is thus to ensure it. If I imagine that, try as I might, I am bound to fail, I shall not even try as I might. But the Christian is forbidden such disastrous pessimism. For Scripture tells him that at conversion the Spirit united him to the living Christ. This was his regeneration. It made him a "new creation" (2 Cor 5:17), and ensured his permanent superiority in the conflict with sin. The Bible describes what then occurred in three complementary ways, each of which from a different angle confirms that this is so.

1. *The Spirit implanted a new life-principle.* As the direct result of union with the risen and living Christ, regeneration is spoken of as being "quickened" or "raised" with him (see Eph 2:6; Col 2:12; 3:1). As the beginning of spiritual life in man, it is spoken of as being "born again" and "begotten of God" (see Jas 1:18; 1 Pt 1:3; 1 Jn 5:18). The dynamic thus implanted is the "new heart" and "new spirit" promised in Ezekiel 36:26, the "new self" put on at conversion (see Eph 4:24), the "seed" of God in his children's hearts (see 1 Jn 3:9). This new energy finds its characteristic expression in the same attitude and relationship to God as that which marked Christ's human life; a spontaneous affinity to God and love for him and for his Word and his people. Faith, love, and opposition to sin are its natural fruits, and sure signs of its presence (see Gal 5:6, 17). The Christian's new nature and true self, the "inner being" that delights in God's laws (see

Rom 7:22), replaces sin as the reigning power in his heart and the dominant impulse in his life. It is no longer his nature to sin. Insofar as he does so, he acts out of character, and his heart is not in it. He can never sin with all his heart again.

2. *The Spirit dealt a deathblow to sin.* This is clear, from what was said above. By our regenerating union with Christ and the incoming of the new life, sin receives a blow from which it can never recover. Its power is broken, and its ultimate destruction guaranteed. Accordingly, God tells his people that "sin will have no dominion over you" (Rom 6:14). Its reign has ended as far as they are concerned. Their part is now by mortification to hasten the demise of their dethroned and doomed enemy. Hereby he assures them that however furious or stubborn sin may prove, however deeply it may have entrenched itself behind habits and temperamental weaknesses, sustained pressure cannot fail to uproot and rout it.

3. *The Spirit took up residence in the heart.* The Spirit now indwells the believer (see Rom 8:9-11; 1 Cor 6:19), to convey life each moment from Christ to him (see Col 2:19) and thus to make the "seed" in his heart grow and bear the Spirit's fruit (see Gal 5:22). The Spirit is present in person to oppose indwelling sin. He teaches the Christian to understand revealed truth and apply it to himself, stirs him up to obey it, and strengthens him as he does so. Where the indwelling Spirit exerts his sovereign power, failure is impossible.

When the Christian fights sin, therefore, he opposes a dethroned and debilitated foe; he is animated by the energy of what is now the deepest and most powerful instinct in his nature; and he goes in the strength of the Holy Spirit of God. His superiority is assured; he may join battle with confidence; he is going to win.

Step 4: We must know how to use our resources. It is true that we could not mortify sin by our own unaided efforts; but it is no less true that the Spirit will not mortify sin in us without our cooperation. He will prosper our striving, but he will not bless our sloth. We ourselves, then, must attack sin; and the outcome of the conflict will depend on whether we fight wisely and make good use of our available strength. The three prime rules for doing so are these:

1. *Grow.* "Growing, thriving, and improving in universal holiness," wrote Owen, "is the great way of the mortification of sin.... The more we abound in the fruits of the Spirit, the less shall we be concerned in the works of the flesh.... This is that which will ruin sin, and without it nothing will contribute anything thereunto." We must nourish our new nature on God's truth and exercise it constantly in prayer, worship, witness, and a consistent, all-around (universal) obedience. We should plan to practice and develop the qualities most contrary to the sins we have to get rid of— generosity if the problem is greed, a habit of praise if it is self-pity, patience and forbearance if it is bad temper, planned living if it is sloth, or whatever. We must forestall sin's attempts to regain control of our hearts and powers by preoccupying ourselves in the active service of God. Feeble Christians, the careless, the half-hearted and the double-minded, can never mortify sin.

2. *Watch.* It is our responsibility to shun temptation as far as we can. To expect God by his sovereign power to kill lusts in us while we read the books and keep the company and expose ourselves to the influences that we know foment them is presumption, not faith, and is more likely to bring down a curse than a blessing. It has been truly said that though you can't stop birds flying over your head, you can

stop them nesting in your hair. We must be ruthless in starving sin of all that feeds it. Mortification is impossible otherwise.

3. *Pray.* Prayer alone obtains help from God. Promises that are not claimed are not normally fulfilled: "you do not have, because you do not ask" (Jas 4:2). The Spirit's help in mortification is gained only by constant believing prayer, as we claim the promise that sin shall not rule us, as we apply again and again to the Lord, who came and died and rose and lives to save us from sin, for "grace to help us in our time of need" (Heb 4:16). If we ask and expect we shall not be disappointed.

God's Words, pp. 185–88

ॐ

Holy Ghost, with pow'r divine,
Cleanse this guilty heart of mine;
Long hath sin without control
Held dominion o'er my soul.

Holy Spirit, all divine,
Dwell within this heart of mine;
Cast down every idol throne,
Reign supreme and reign alone.

ॐ

ANDREW REED

12

Christian Character Reigns Supreme

We are children of an age that values kicks above character, self-gratification above self-control, and emotional development above moral stature. Pleasures are regarded as more important than fidelity or honesty or altruism or service, and we plan harder for recreation than we do for righteousness. Not surprisingly, Christian folk catch this spirit (or it catches them) and in the Church they seek a whirl of excitement, emotional "highs," novelties, psychedelic therapies, thrilling intimacies of fellowship, shouting preachers, stirring songs, everything constantly on the boil; and they easily forget that God's priority is character rather than kicks, and his aim in dealing with us is our holiness, from which our happiness, in the sense of contentment with the way things are, flows as a by-product. But so it is, and the feverish state of mind that has just been described is not good health, spiritually. Seeking holiness in Christ must come first, and the practice of mortifying sin, first by maintaining a daily crucifying of the flesh (see Gal 5:24) and then by watching and praying in order to drain the life out of the particular "passions of the flesh that wage war against your soul" (1 Pt 2:11), is an essential element in that quest. More Christlikeness of character is the only sure sign of spiritual progress.

We know that holiness is a priority; we seek to maintain our first repentance by daily consecration; we want to walk worthy of our calling each day of our lives. But we find in ourselves what, from the biblical standpoint, we must call habits of moral failure—jealousy, envy, greed, impatience, apathy, lust (heterosexual and homosexual), self-absorption, sloth, apathy, indiscipline, festering resentment, discontent, arrogance, offhandedness, and so on. What are we to do about it? Such habits are like running sores in our spiritual lives: they have to be broken and replaced with appropriate facets of the moral image of Jesus. But how?

There is no magic formula for instant replacement of unChristlike habits by their opposite. Joyous inward experiences of God's presence and love, fulfilling the promise of John 14:21, 23, may strengthen your motivation for cleaving to God (see Rom 12:1), and have been known to snuff out the insistent obsessive cravings (for alcohol, drugs, tobacco, gambling) that were fueled by self-hatred: a fact that has sometimes led to these revelations of love being misconceived as experiences of sanctification. In fact, however, when the experience is over the need to seek character change still remains, and it is only by self-knowledge, self-discipline, self-watch, and self-distrustful prayer in face of temptation and the recurring routines of sinful habits that headway here will be made. Gifted and electrifying people with flaws in their moral system are top-heavy, and riding for a fall; they should not be taken as role models. As regular exercise is needed to maintain good physical health, so fighting and winning the battle for Christian character through the imitation of Christ and the mortification of sin is the regular exercise by which alone good spiritual health is maintained.

Paul really makes this very clear: so clear that we are much to blame if we evade the issue.

> You have died, and now the life you have is hidden with Christ in God. But when Christ is revealed—and he is your life—you too will be revealed in all your glory with him.
>
> That is why you must kill [mortify] everything in you that belongs only to earthly life: fornication, impurity, guilty passion, evil desires and especially greed ... give all these things up: getting angry, being bad-tempered, spitefulness, abusive language and dirty talk; and never tell each other lies. You have stripped off your old behavior with your old self, and you have put on a new self which will progress towards true

knowledge the more it is renewed in the image of its creator; and in that image ... there is only Christ: he is everything and he is in everything.

COLOSSIANS 3:3-11, JB

God's Words, pp. 188–90

ᴣ

Blest are the pure in heart,
For they shall see our God;
The secret of the Lord is theirs,
Their soul is Christ's abode.

The Lord, who left the heavens
Our life and peace to bring,
To dwell in lowliness with men,
Their pattern and their King;

Still to the lowly soul
He doth himself impart,
And for his dwelling and his throne
Chooses the pure in heart.

Lord, I thy presence seek,
May mine this blessing be;
Give me a pure and lowly heart,
A temple meet for thee.

ᴣ

J. KEBLE

Suffering Is Not for Nothing

ॐ

13

Expect Suffering

Suffering (getting what one does not want while wanting what one does not get) is specified in Scripture as part of every Christian's calling, and therefore of mine as much as of anyone else's. (Authors who write about life are not therefore excused from the task of actually living it!) Suffering must be expected, and even valued, by all believers without exception.

God does not shield Christians from the world's ill will. Just by living as they do, finding their dignity and delight in pleasing God and dissociating themselves from the self-serving rat race that the devotees of pleasure, profit, and power spend their whole life running, Christians condemn the world (see Eph 5:8-14; Heb 11:7). The world, stung, retaliates with anti-Christian anger. So to his disciples Jesus says: "If the world hates you, keep in mind that it hated me first. If you belonged to the world, it would love you ... but I have chosen you out of the world. That is why the world hates you" (Jn 15:18-19; see 1 Pt 4:4; 1 Jn 3:13). Whether the world's hostility is casual or focused, whether it is contemptuous and cool or flaming and ferocious, whether it is expressed in official persecution or informal cold-shouldering and social ostracism, it is always there as a more or less resentful reaction to people who—because of their prior loyalty—decline, albeit peacefully, to fit into the conventions, lifestyle, and value system that are felt in some way to hold the community together.

Nor does God shield his children from personal traumas and troubles: losses and crosses, as the Puritans used to call them. On the contrary! In this fallen world, where the entry of sin has put everything out of joint, Jesus the Redeemer experienced trouble—an uncomprehending family, a hostile civil authority, friends who failed him—and the redeemed who follow him now find themselves in the same boat. Christians, like Jesus, get betrayed and victimized, as we have seen already. Christians get swindled and forced into bankruptcy, like others. Christians have family troubles, as others do. All seems well, then suddenly someone has cancer, someone is jailed, someone has become permanently and agonizingly dependent, someone who should not be pregnant is pregnant, someone has AIDS, one's child has died, one's spouse walks out on one. That is just a sample list of things that happen. One is left feeling that the roof has fallen in, and one is utterly alone and ruined, much as Job must have felt on his ash heap. (And Christians, too, find themselves, like Job, having to endure at such times the censures of self-righteous know-alls, which make the pain worse.)

Other burrs under our saddle come, not from our relational involvements, but from our lack of a healthy body or a healthy mind. There are, for instance, Christians who battle throughout their adult lives with homosexual cravings that they know it is wrong to indulge, but that nag incessantly. In the same way, constant struggling with any other obsessive urge that others do not share (sadism, for instance, or the passion to pilfer) is painful. But we were never promised that living uprightly would be an easy business. Ease is for heaven, not earth. Life on earth is fundamentally out of shape and out of order by reason of sin. The God who loves and saves sinners has chosen to let life go on that way most of the time. So strains, pains, disappointments, traumas, and frustrations of all sorts await us in the future, just as they have overtaken us already in the past. Suffering is to be expected, and we must prepare for it. It is a biblically predicted fact of every Christian's life that our joys will be punctuated with bad experiences to the very end.

Does that thought startle you? It should not. The world, of course, does not find value in suffering. It has no reason to. But

Christians are in a different position, for the Bible assures us that God sanctifies our suffering to good ends. We are not to pretend, out of stoical pride, that we feel no pain or distress. Equally, however, we are not to spend all our time brooding on how we suffer, for that is sinful self-absorption. In any case, there are more important things to do. Our task is to take suffering in stride, not as if it is a pleasure (it isn't), but in the knowledge that God will not let it overwhelm us and that he will use it.

Rediscovering Holiness, pp. 251–55

In thy strength I rest me;
Foes who would molest me
Cannot reach me here.
Though the earth be shaking,
Every heart be quaking,
God dispels our fear.
Sin and hell in conflict fell
With their heaviest storms assail us:
Jesus will not fail us.

Banished is our sadness!
For the Lord of gladness,
Jesus, enters in.
Those who love the Father
Tho' the storms may gather,
Still have peace within.
Yea whate'er we here must bear,
Still in thee lies purest pleasure,
Jesus, priceless treasure!

JOHANN FRANCK
TRANSLATED BY CATHERINE WINKWORTH

14

The School of Holiness

It is reported that on one occasion when Teresa of Avila was traveling, her conveyance dumped her in the mud. The spunky saint's first words as she struggled to her feet were: "Lord, if this is how you treat your friends, it is no wonder that you have so few!" One of the most attractive things about Teresa is that she could be playful like this with her God. But none knew better than she that the ups and downs of her life were divinely planned in order to mold her character, enlarge her heart, and deepen her devotion. And what was true for her is true for us all.

In God's school of holiness our Lord Jesus Christ (the Father's Son and the Christian's Savior) is with us, and we with him, in a controlling relationship of master and servant, leader and follower, teacher and student. It is crucially important to appreciate this. Why is it that in the school of holiness, as in the schools to which we send our own children, some move ahead faster than others? How are the different rates of progress to be explained? Fundamentally, the factor that makes the difference is neither one's intelligence quotient nor the number of books one has read nor the conferences, camps, and seminars one has attended, but the quality of the fellowship with Christ that one maintains through life's vicissitudes.

Jesus is risen. He is alive and well. Through his Word and Spirit he calls us to himself today, to receive him as our Savior and Lord and become his disciples and followers. Speaking objectively—with reference to how things really are, as distinct from how they might feel at any particular moment—the "there-ness" of Jesus, and the personal nature of his relationship with us as his disciples, are as truly matters of fact as were his bodily presence and his words of comfort and command when he walked this earth long ago. Some, however, do not reckon with this fact as robustly and practically as others do. This is what makes the difference.

I mean this. Some who trust Jesus as their Savior have formed the habit of going to him about everything that comes up, in order to become clear on how they should react to it as his disciples. ("Going to him" is an umbrella phrase that covers three things: praying; meditating, which includes thinking, reflecting, drawing conclusions from Scripture, and applying them directly to oneself in Jesus' presence; and holding oneself open throughout the process to specific illumination from the Holy Spirit.) These Christians come to see how events are requiring them to:

- consecrate themselves totally to the Father, as Jesus did;
- say and do only what pleases the Father, as Jesus did;
- accept pain, grief, disloyalty, and betrayal, as Jesus did;
- care for people and serve their needs without either compromise of principle or ulterior motives in practice, as Jesus did;
- accept opposition and isolation, hoping patiently for better things and meantime staying steady under pressure, as Jesus did;
- rejoice in the specifics of the Father's ways and thank him for his wisdom and goodness, as Jesus did;
  and so on.

Kept by this means from bitterness and self-pity, these Christians cope with events in a spirit of peace, joy, and eagerness to see what God will do next. Others, however, who are no less committed to Jesus as their Savior, never master this art of habitually going to him about life's challenges. Too often they start by assuming that their life as children of God will be a bed of roses all the way. Then when the storms come, the best they can do is stagger through in a spirit of real if unacknowledged disappointment with God, feeling all the time that he has let them down. It is easy to understand why those in the first category advance farther and faster in the love, joy, humility, and hope that form the essence of Christlike holiness than those in the second category.

Rediscovering Holiness, pp. 15–19

৵

Be still, my soul! the Lord is on thy side;
Bear patiently the cross of grief or pain;
Leave to thy God to order and provide;
In every change he faithful will remain.
Be still, my soul! thy best, thy heavenly Friend
Thro' thorny ways leads to a joyful end.

Be still, my soul! thy God doth undertake
To guide the future as he has the past.
Thy hope, thy confidence, let nothing shake;
All now mysterious shall be bright at last.
Be still, my soul! the waves and wind still know
His voice who ruled them while he dwelt below.

৵

KATHARINA VON SCHLEGEL
TRANSLATED BY JANE L. BORTHWICK

15

Troubles Lead to Glory

"We can be full of joy here and now even in our trials and troubles," writes Paul. "Taken in the right spirit these very things will give us patient endurance; this in turn will develop as mature character, and a character of this sort produces a steady hope" (Rom 5:3-4.; see Jas 1:2-4). How this works is explained in Hebrews 12:5-11. The writer, having urged his readers to run life's race with eyes fixed on Jesus and no yielding to sin, goes on to tell them that their pains and griefs are their heavenly Father's moral training, inflicted not out of brutal indifference but in order to lick them into a holy shape. "Endure hardship as discipline; God is treating you as sons. For what son is not disciplined by his father?... God disciplines us for our good, that we may share in his holiness. No discipline seems pleasant at the time, but painful. Later on, however, it produces a harvest of righteousness and peace for those who have been trained by it" (Heb 12:7, 10-11). Scars tie in with sanctity. Pain has an educational effect.

Educational pain? How savage it sounds! But how realistic the point really is! "What son is not disciplined by his father?" Parents who love their children take time out to discipline them when young, so that they may one day be adults that the parents can be proud of. This is simply true. The fact is that without the holiness that comes through God's discipline, "no one will see the Lord" (v.14). But if God is taking the trouble to train us up in righteousness here and now, that shows that he is preparing us for an eternity of joy with our Lord Jesus at his right hand. This is how our holy Father in heaven works for our good.

The divine education that is in view here has two sides. One was expressed by George Whitefield, the eighteenth-century evangelist, who spoke somewhere of our kindly Lord putting thorns in all our beds lest, like the disciples in Gethsemane, we be found sleeping when we need to be watching and praying. As bodily discomfort keeps us awake physically, so lack of situational ease and contentment will keep us awake spiritually.

The other side is revealed by Jesus' summons to every would-be disciple to "deny himself and take up his cross daily and follow me" (Lk 9:23, cf. 14:27). The only persons in Jesus' day who carried their own crosses were condemned criminals from the slave and non-Roman-citizen classes who had to walk to the place of their crucifixion. These were persons who had lost their civil rights, whom society had decreed that it wanted dead, and at whose imminent sufferings—and crucifixion, remember, was the cruelest form of execution ever devised—no one was going to turn a hair. Jesus, at the end of his life, literally joined that category. But what he was saying in the words quoted was that morally he was in it already, by virtue of people's negative attitude of heart toward him. His followers, then, must clear-headedly accept a similar outcast relationship to the community around them, because that is all they can expect if they are loyal to him.

This is what self-denial really means—not a mere cutting back on some bit of private self-indulgence, but totally surrendering one's natural wish for acceptance and status and respect. It means preparing to be rejected as worthless and dispensable, and to find oneself robbed of one's rights.

The Greek word that Phillips, the New International Version, and many others translate as "character" in Romans 5:4 is *dokimē*. Strictly speaking, this term expresses the complex thought of proven quality recognized and approved as such by an interested party—in this case, God himself. The reason why *dokimē* brings hope (confidence that joy and glory with Christ will be one's ultimate inheritance) is not that persons who have stood fast through thick and thin may now pass votes of confidence in themselves, but that the God whom they serve generates within them an awareness that in his strength they have passed tests that he himself imposed. Their patience in showing loyalty to him under the pressure they endured was his own gift to them, and it has left them stronger than they were before. Christians who have gone through hardship for their Lord's sake are tested products of proven quality. *Dokimē* signifies this state of triumphant testedness, with God's seal of approval marking it.

Now *dokimē*, says Paul, produces hope. Our sense of the glory of the life to come is sharpened, and our longing for it is intensified, both as a spontaneous spinoff of the knowledge of God's present approval and as a direct fruit of knowing that the agony has actually enlarged our capacity to enjoy the final glory when it comes. Paul is explicit about this in 2 Corinthians 4:17-18, where writing out of a spell of life-threatening experiences (see 1:8-10), he says, not in irony, but expressing his honest retrospective assessment of what he had been through: "Our light [!] and momentary troubles are achieving for us an eternal glory that far outweighs them all. So we fix our eyes not on what is seen, but on what is unseen. For what is seen is temporary, but what is unseen is eternal." Paul does not, of course, mean that suffering earns glory in the way that work earns a status. He means only to imply that suffering makes one more able to enjoy the coming glory than one was before, just as one enjoys renewed bodily health more when it has been preceded by much sickness and pain. Integral to the Christlikeness of character that the Refiner's fire of suffering induces is a deepening passion of joyful hope, and hopeful joy.

Rediscovering Holiness, pp. 255–58

My hope is built on nothing less
Than Jesus' blood and righteousness;
I dare not trust the sweetest frame,
But wholly lean on Jesus' name.

When darkness veils his lovely face,
I rest on his unchanging grace;
In every high and stormy gale,
My anchor holds within the veil.

His oath, his covenant, his blood,
Support me in the whelming flood;
When all around my soul gives way,
He then is all my hope and stay.

EDWARD MOTE

16

God's Power Is Shown in Human Weakness

There are many sorts of weakness. There is the bodily weakness of the invalid or cripple; there is the character weakness of the person with besetting shortcomings and vices; there is the intellectual weakness of the person with limited ability; there is the weakness brought on by exhaustion, depression, stress, strain, and emotional overload. God sanctifies all these forms of weakness by enabling the weak to be stronger (more patient, more outgoing, more affectionate, more tranquil, more joyful, and more resourceful) than seemed possible under the circumstances. This is a demonstration of his power that he delights to give.

Paul states the principle thus: "We have this treasure [knowledge of God in Christ] in jars of clay to show that the all-surpassing power is from God and not from us. We are hard pressed on every side, but not crushed; perplexed, but not in despair; persecuted, but not abandoned; struck down, but not destroyed. We always carry around in our body the death of Jesus, so that the life of Jesus may also be revealed in our body.... So then, death is at work in us" (2 Cor 4:7-10, 12). In a self-centered, pleasure-oriented, self-indulgent world like ours today, this sounds most brutal and chilling. But it is, in fact, the true meaning of the time-honored, much-applauded dictum, "Man's extremity is God's opportunity." Opportunity for what?—to show his power, the power of his grace, now displayed for the praise of his glory.

Being weak, and feeling weak, is not in itself fun, nor can it be a condition of what the world would see as maximum efficiency. One might have expected God to use his power to eliminate such weakness from the lives of his servants. In fact, however, what he does again and again is to make his weak servants into walking wonders—sometimes, of course, in the physical sense, immobilized wonders—of wisdom, love, and helpfulness to others despite their disability. It is thus that he loves to show his power. This is a truth that is vitally important to understand. Paul himself learned this lesson very thoroughly through his interaction with the Corinthians. Paul was not a man for half measures, self-effacement, or standoff relationships. He was naturally a "ball of fire," as we say, imperious, combative, brilliant, and passionate. Conscious of his apostolic authority and very sure that his teaching was definitive and health-giving, he spent himself unstintingly in the discipling of his converts. He felt and expressed deep affection for them because they were Christ's, and naturally looked not only for obedience but also for affection in return.

In the case of the Corinthians, however, the obedience was wavering and grudging, and the affection was virtually nil. This, as Paul's letters to them illustrate, was partly because Paul did not come up to their conceited expectation that any teacher worth his salt would throw his intellectual weight about in order to impress them. It was partly, too, because other teachers, who did throw their weight about, had secured their loyalty, and partly also because they had embraced a triumphalist view of spiritual life that valued tongue-speaking and uninhibitedness above love, humility, and righteousness. They thought of Christians as persons set free by Christ to do just about anything, with no regard for the consequences. They looked down on Paul as "weak"—unimpressive in presence and in speech (see 2 Cor 10:10), and possibly wrong in some of his doctrinal and moral teaching. They were very critical of his personal style and behavior.

Anyone in Paul's position would find this painful to a degree, and it is clear from his letters to the Corinthians, with their expressions of anguished love and their alternations of pain, anger, disappointment, frustration, and sarcasm, that Paul himself did find it exceedingly painful. His response, however, was magnificent. He embraced weakness—not the weakness of ministry alleged by the Corinthians, but the weakness of a sick body, a servant role, and a hurting heart—as his calling here on earth. "If I must boast," he wrote, "I will boast of the things that show my weakness" (2 Cor 11:30). "I will not boast about myself, except about my weaknesses" (2 Cor 12:5).

Rediscovering Holiness, pp. 232–38

꿍

I am weak but thou art strong;

Jesus, keep me from all wrong;

I'll be satisfied as long

As I walk, let me walk close to thee.

꿍

TRADITIONAL FOLK SONG

17

Thorns

To keep me from becoming conceited ... there was given me a thorn in my flesh, a messenger of Satan, to torment me. Three times I pleaded with the Lord to take it away from me. But he said to me, "My grace is sufficient for you, for my power is made perfect in weakness." Therefore I will boast all the more gladly about my weaknesses, so that Christ's power may rest on me. That is why, for Christ's sake, I delight in weaknesses, in insults, in hardships, in persecutions, in difficulties. For when I am weak, then I am strong.

2 CORINTHIANS 12:7-10

What was the apostle Paul's thorn? We do not know. But it must have been a personal disability, some malfunctioning in his makeup, or he would not have said it was in his "flesh" (meaning his created humanity). And it must have been painful, or he would not have called it a "thorn."

Why did Paul pray specifically to the Lord Jesus about his thorn? Because Jesus was the Healer, who had wrought many miraculous cures in the days of his flesh and some through Paul during Paul's years of missionary ministry (see Acts 14:3, 8-10; 19:11). Now Paul needed Christ's healing power for himself, so in three solemn seasons of prayer he sought it.

Why was healing withheld? Not for lack of pure-hearted prayer on Paul's part, nor for lack of sovereign power on Christ's part, but because the Savior had something better in view for his servant. (God always reserves the right to answer our requests in a better way than we make them.) Jesus' response to Paul's prayer could be expanded like this: "Paul, I will tell you what I am going to do. I am going to display my strength in your continuing weakness, in such a way that the things you fear—the ending or enfeebling of your ministry, the loss of your credibility and usefulness—will not occur. Your ministry will go on in power and strength as before, though in greater weakness than before. You will carry this thorn in the flesh with you as long as you live. But in that condition of weakness, my strength will be made perfect. It will become more obvious than ever that it is I who keep you going." The implication was that this state of things would be more to Paul's personal blessing, more to the enriching of his ministry, and more to the glory of Christ the Enabler, than an immediate cure would be.

Paul's experience certainly is a model to which we again and again find ourselves required to conform. The pattern is that the Lord first makes us conscious of our weakness, so that our heart cries out, "I can't handle this." We go to the Lord to ask him to remove the burden that we feel is crushing us. But Christ replies: "In my strength you *can* handle this, and in answer to your prayer, I will *strengthen* you to handle it." Thus in the end our testimony, like Paul's, is: "I can do everything through him who gives me strength" (Phil 4:13); "The Lord stood at my side and gave me strength" (2 Tm 4:17). And we find ourselves saying, with Paul: "Praise be to the God and Father of our Lord Jesus Christ, the Father of compassion and the God of all comfort, who comforts us in all our troubles, so that we can comfort those in any trouble with the comfort we ourselves have received from God. For just as the sufferings of Christ flow over into our lives, so also through Christ our comfort overflows" (2 Cor 1:3-5).

By "comfort," Paul means the encouragement that invigorates, not the relaxation that enervates. It is in that sense that we join him in testifying to the comfort of God. We find ourselves living (if I may put it this way) baptismally, with resurrection-out-of-death as the recurring shape of our experience. And we realize with ever-growing clarity that this is the fullest and pro-foundest expression of the empowered Christian life.

It appears, then, that being divinely empowered so that one grows stronger in Christ has nothing necessarily to do with per-forming spectacularly or, by human standards, successfully (whether or not one performs so is for God to decide). It has everything to do, however, with knowing and feeling that one is weak. In this sense, we only grow stronger by growing weaker. The world means by strength (of character, mind, and will) a natural endowment, the ability to press ahead, undistracted and undiscouraged, toward one's goals. God-given strength or power is, however, a matter of being enabled by Christ himself through the Spirit to keep on keeping on, however weak one feels. One keeps on even in situations where what is being asked for seems to be beyond one, and one does so in the confidence that this is how God means it to be. For only at the point where the insufficiency of natural strength is faced, felt, and admitted does divine empowering begin.

Rediscovering Holiness, pp. 232–38

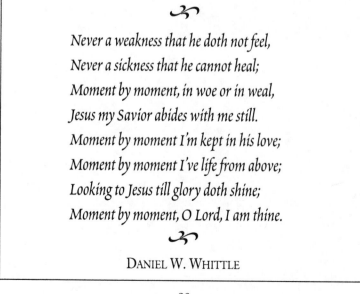

Never a weakness that he doth not feel,
Never a sickness that he cannot heal;
Moment by moment, in woe or in weal,
Jesus my Savior abides with me still.
Moment by moment I'm kept in his love;
Moment by moment I've life from above;
Looking to Jesus till glory doth shine;
Moment by moment, O Lord, I am thine.

DANIEL W. WHITTLE

18

Endurance

The colloquial English word for endurance is "stickability." Its North American counterpart is "stick-to-itiveness."

Endurance is a major New Testament theme. And patience (the passive mode of endurance, whereby pain, grief, suffering, and disappointment are handled without inner collapse) is named as one facet, if we may so speak, of the fruit of the Spirit (see Gal 5:22-23). This means that it is not a natural endowment but a supernatural gift, a grace of character that God imparts to those whom he is transforming into the likeness of Christ.

Patient endurance is most apparent when we stand steady under pain and pressure instead of cutting and running, or crumpling and collapsing. But hanging tough in this way is a habit that takes some learning. The hardness of the gaining that produces Christian character must not be minimized: to endure Christianly (which means, in fruit-of-the-Spirit terms, lovingly, joyfully, peacefully, kindly, without loss of goodness, faithfulness, gentleness, and self-control) is no casual agenda. Many of us have hardly begun to tackle it as yet. Integral to our holiness, our maturity and our Christlikeness, however, is this habit of enduring. Forming the habit, and making sure we never lose it, is a necessary discipline for those who are Christ's.

The life of Christian endurance is like a long-distance race. The race picture in the New Testament (see Heb 12:1-3; 1 Cor 9:24-27; Gal 5:7; Phil 2:16; 2 Tm 4:7) is telling us two things: first, that perseverance is the only path to the prize of final glory and, second, that what perseverance requires is a sustained exertion of concentrated effort day in and day out—a single-minded, wholehearted, self-denying, flat-out commitment to praising and pleasing the Father through the Son as long as life lasts.

This sustained inward effort is fueled by a heart of joy as the winning-post appears ahead. Real Jesus-likeness means this— nothing less.

The life of Christian endurance is lived by fixing our eyes on Jesus. "Fixing our eyes" is a good translation (see Heb 12:2). The Greek word implies that one looks away from everything else in order to concentrate on one's object of attention. Christians are surrounded, sometimes almost deafened, by the siren songs of those who want them to stop being awkward customers who behave Christianly and become worldly wimps who do only what those around them are already doing. Christians must learn to disregard these distracting noises. We cannot follow Christ in holiness unless we are willing to stand out from the crowd and swim against the streams.

The secret of endurance, says the writer, is to concentrate on Jesus himself: "look to" him, as the older translations put it; "gaze steadily at him" is the thought that is being expressed. He is the great exemplar of saying "no" to sin at all costs, even at the cost of life itself. His example is there for us to follow (cf. Heb 12:4).

The most vital truth for the life of holy endurance is not, however, that Jesus is our standard. The most vital truth is, rather, that Jesus is our sustainer, our strength for action, our sovereign grace-giver (see Heb 2:18; 4:16), "the author and perfecter of our faith" (Heb 12:2). Faith is a compound of knowing, trusting, hoping, and stubbornly persisting in trust-ful hope against all odds. Faith can do this, the writer implies throughout, because the One who has graciously brought us to faith, and whom we now trust, helps us to do it. "God has said, 'Never will I leave you; never will I forsake you' [Dt 31:6]. So we say with confidence, 'The Lord is my helper ...' [Ps 118:7]" (Heb 13:5-6). "Let us then approach the throne of grace with confidence, so that we may receive mercy and find grace to help us in our time of need" (Heb 4:16).

This confident, expectant approach is faith in action. It is precisely the glorified Lord Jesus, who by his Word and Spirit brought our faith into being and keeps it in being (that is the meaning of "author and perfecter"), who now helps us to stand steady as we gaze on him and cling to him by means of our focused, intentional, heartfelt prayer. It is often said that "help!" is the best prayer anyone ever makes. When directed to the Lord Jesus, it is certainly the most effective. And that last statement (be it said) remains as true for us now as ever it was for anyone, since, as the writer goes on to say, "Jesus Christ is the same yesterday and today and forever" (Heb 13:8).

Rediscovering Holiness, pp. 239–44

ॐ

Every day the Lord himself is near me
With a special mercy for each hour;
All my care he fain would bear, and cheer me,
He whose name is Counsellor and Power.
The protection of his child and treasure
Is a charge that on himself he laid;
"As your days, your strength shall be in measure,"
This the pledge to me he made.

Help me then in every tribulation
So to trust your promises, O Lord,
That I lose not faith's sweet consolation
Offered me within your holy Word.
Help me, Lord, when toil and trouble meeting,
E'er to take, as from a father's hand,
One by one, the days, the moments fleeting,
Till I reach the promised land.

ॐ

CAROLINE SANDELL BERG
TRANSLATED BY ANDREW L. SKOOG

19

Our Suffering Glorifies God

"Glory" means God's display to his creatures of the perfections that are his—the wisdom, power, uprightness, and love that, singly and combined, make him praiseworthy. Further, he is "glorified" when by word and deed he shows these qualities to his rational creatures. "Glory" also means the praise that our thanks, trust, adoration, submission, and devotion give to God, for the praiseworthiness we have now seen in him. He is "glorified" when we exalt him responsively in these ways.

In times of weakness and woe, Christianly handled, God is glorified in both senses. On the one hand, he reveals the glorious riches of his resources in Christ by keeping us going, so that overwhelming pressures do not overwhelm us, even when they look like doing so. The apostle Paul explains that God's purpose in these pressures is to make apparent to all the supernatural power of Christ's risen life and gracious enabling, whereby saints are kept going in situations where it seemed impossible that anyone could keep going (see 2 Cor 4:8-9; 6:9-10).

Nor is this a special experience reserved for special people in the family of God. On the contrary, it is a matter of promise to all God's people. That is implied by Paul's word to the Corinthians: "No temptation has seized you except what is common to man. And God is faithful; he will not let you be tempted beyond what you can bear. But when you are tempted, he will also provide a way out so that you can stand up under it" (1 Cor 10:13). Temptations are places and times of decision in which

Satan works to bring us down in an experience of defeat while God acts to build us up through an experience of overcoming. The pain, grief, self-hatred, disappointment, fear, and inner exhaustion that are so often part of the temptation experience isolate us from the seemingly untroubled. They make us feel that what we face and experience is worse than what has ever confronted anyone else before. But it never is so; and there will always be "grace to help us in our time of need" whenever we seek it (Heb 4:16). Whatever the burden, the power is there to keep the Christian from crumpling. Through God's faithfulness in supplying supernatural strength to those who are in Christ, they endure hardship, overcome temptation, and keep going as before, and in them God glorifies himself mightily.

The other side of the matter is modeled by psalm after psalm and by Paul and Silas singing hymns in their cell with their feet in the stocks after their flogging at Philippi (see Acts 16:23-25). The proper response to pressure is praise plus prayer. The fiercer the opposition, the stronger the praise should be. It is through praise no less than through petition that help comes. It is by praise over and above petition that we most directly honor and glorify God, out of the depths and in the fire no less than at quieter times. Praise brings strength to endure, even as it gives glory to God our strengthener.

Richard Baxter was an English Puritan, and like most of the English Puritans, he suffered for much of his life through bad housing and bad health; community hostility; social ostracism; political, ecclesiastical, and economic upsets; and actual persecution. The Puritans grasped (as many of us today do not) that Christians are not called to be the nicest people in the world according to the world's idea of what a nice person is like. Instead, they are to be the Lord's counterculture, living with different motives, purposes, and values from those of the world because of their loyalty to God. When Christians behave in a way that society finds odd and judgmental (and Christians do not have to be actually judgmental before they are felt to be such), society will soon gang up against them in one way or another. The Puritans experienced this—hence the malicious stereotypes of Puritans that still go the rounds among people who ought to know better—and consistent Christians experience it still. John Geree, describing the character of an old English Puritan in 1646, pictured this model man as having for his motto *Vincit qui patitur,* "he who suffers conquers." It really does seem that of all Protestants since the Reformation the Puritans had as hard a furrow to plow as any. But Baxter was not the only Puritan who, following the lead of David in Psalm 34:1, praised the Lord at all times, and who by this discipline (which was also, for the Puritans, a delight, as it can be for us too) persistently glorified God. In doing so he found strength to stand fast in God's service.

Rediscovering Holiness, pp. 259–62

Ye saints, who toil below,
Adore your heavenly King,
And onward as ye go
Some joyful anthem sing.
Take what he gives
And praise him still,
Through good and ill,
Who ever lives!

My soul, bear thou thy part,
Triumph in God above,
And with a well-tuned heart
Sing thou the songs of love!
Let all thy days
Till life shall end,
Whate'er he send,
Be filled with praise.

RICHARD BAXTER

20

Life From Death

Before there is blessing anywhere, there will first be suffering somewhere. Jesus first announced this law when he declared, speaking of his own ministry, "Unless a kernel of wheat falls to the ground and dies, it remains only a single seed. But if it dies, it produces many seeds" (Jn 12:24). The many seeds in his case were the many millions for whom his cross would mean new life. Then, having said (v.25) that following him requires willingness to lay down one's life, he declared: "Whoever serves me must follow me" (v. 26). The natural implication is that he requires all who are his to live by the same law of harvest that he lived by himself, becoming the seed that dies to bring forth fruit. Every experience of pain, grief, frustration, disappointment, and being hurt by others is a little death. When we serve the Savior in our worldly world, there are many such deaths to be died. But the call to us is to endure, since God sanctifies our endurance for fruitfulness in the lives of others.

Paul's grasp of this principle is reflected in several of his remarks about his own ministry. "I rejoice in what was suffered for you" ("my sufferings for your sake," RSV). Also, he says, "I fill up in my flesh what is still lacking in regard to Christ's afflictions, for the sake of his body, which is the church" (Col 1:24). Paul is affirming a link between his troubles (he was writing from prison) and the furtherance of Christ's work of building his Church. To the Corinthians he writes: "Death is at work in us, but life is at work in you" (2 Cor 4:12). To Timothy he writes:

"I endure everything for the sake of the elect, that they too may obtain the salvation that is in Christ Jesus, with eternal glory" (2 Tm 2:10). In each of these texts, the reality of a connection between his own suffering and others being blessed is made clear, though the nature of the connection is not precisely defined.

Part of the meaning of the principle, surely—even if not all—is that through the pounding we experience we are, so to speak, broken up small so that each bit of what we are may become food for some hungry soul: food, that is, in the sense of empathetic insight and supportive wisdom. In ministry to others it is often decisively helpful when we can say: "I know how you are feeling. I've been there myself. And God met me there and taught me lessons and saw me through—let me tell you about it." As Jesus once explained that the reason a man was born blind was not punishment for anyone's past sin, but God's present purpose of displaying divine power by healing him (see Jn 9:1-3), so the true answer to the question, "Why is this happening to me?" will often be: It is not chastening or correction for yesterday's moral lapses. It has nothing to do with the past at all. It has to do only with the use God plans to make of you tomorrow, and how you need to be prepared for that. The hard and bitter experiences that now ravage you, like the death of a loved one (one example), are fitting you to be a channel of God's life to someone else. So you should expect hardship in some form to continue all your days, according to Jesus' own declaration: "Every branch [in me, the vine] that does bear fruit he [the Father] prunes so that it will be even more fruitful" (Jn 15:2). That is how the law of harvest works.

We see that law further illustrated in Isaiah 50:4-9, one of the servant-songs that point prophetically ahead to the suffering and glory of Jesus. This song is in the first instance Isaiah's own testimony. It begins: "The sovereign Lord has given me an instructed tongue, to know the word that sustains the weary." It continues: "I offered my back to those who beat me, my cheeks to those who pulled out my beard; I did not hide my face from mocking and spitting.... It is the sovereign Lord who helps me...." The implication is that the word that sustains the weary only comes to be known through the experience of others' hatred and brutality. Isaiah juxtaposes these two things because they are parts of a single package.

Even more clearly is the fruitfulness of suffering for ministry illustrated by the experience of our Lord Jesus himself. Jesus "has been tempted in every way, just as we are—yet was without sin" (Heb 4:15), and now as a result "is able to help those who are being tempted" (Heb 2:18). The strain he underwent in enduring temptation (think of his days in the desert at the start of his ministry, and his hours in Gethsemane at its end) has fitted him to minister help to our harried souls in a way that would not otherwise be a reality. If this was the way the Master went, it is less wonder that his servants should find themselves treading it too.

Rediscovering Holiness, pp. 262–66

꙳

Behold him, ye that pass him by,
The bleeding Prince of life and peace!
Come, sinners, see your Maker die,
And say, was ever grief like his?
Come, feel with me his blood applied:
My Lord, my Love, is crucified.

Then let us sit beneath his cross,
And gladly catch the healing stream,
All things for him account but loss,
And give up all our hearts to him.
Of nothing think or speak beside:
My Lord, my Love, is crucified.

꙳

CHARLES WESLEY

21

Fortitude: Courage With Endurance

Fortitude is bravery and more. Bravery can be fitful and can fade, but fortitude is a compound of courage and endurance. It lasts. Faith fosters fortitude by holding before us our promised hope (see 1 Cor 15:58; Heb 3:6; 6:19-20; 10:23-25; 12:1-13).

Faith also fosters fortitude by realistically receiving God's assurances that pain and strife must be expected in our pilgrimage, and then by inducing purity of heart in those who are actually under pressure and suffering distress. This purity, which is also referred to in Scripture as the simplicity of a united heart and a single eye, is advanced by the experience of affliction. Dr. Samuel Johnson, the eighteenth-century wiseacre of England, once observed that when a man knows he is going to be hanged in a fortnight it concentrates his mind wonderfully. For Christians an awareness that the life God is leading them into is the spiritual counterpart of Winston Churchill's "blood, toil, tears, and sweat" has a similar effect. The world's allurements become much less alluring, and they know with great clarity of mind that a close walk with the Father and the Son, leaning hard on them and drawing strength from them through the Holy Spirit, is both what they need and what they want. Thus in situations of suffering faith purifies the heart.

Three verses from Psalm 119 testify to this. "Before I was afflicted I went astray, but now I obey your word" (v.67). Rough experiences, which could in themselves indicate divine displeasure, challenge us to repent of past thoughtlessness and carelessness and to become more conscientious in doing our Father's will. "It was good for me to be afflicted so that I might learn your decrees" (v.71). As if to say: I did not see clearly what you want for my life, nor what the behavioral model that the Bible spells out for me really involves, until trouble struck me. But I understand it better now. And finally: "I know, O Lord, that ... in faithfulness you have afflicted me" (v.75). God's faithfulness consists in his unwillingness that his children should lose any of the depths of fellowship with himself that he has in store for them. So he afflicts us to make us lean harder on him, in order that his purpose of drawing us into closest fellowship with himself may be fulfilled.

Let me give you two examples of the fortitude that is integral to holiness. The first is Mabel, a blind, deaf, disease-ridden, and cancerous old lady of eighty-nine whom Tom Schmidt met in a convalescent home where she had been bedridden for twenty-five years. He asked her what she thought about as she passed her lonely days and nights. "She said, *I think about Jesus....* I asked, *What do you think about Jesus?* She replied slowly and deliberately as I wrote. And this is what she said: *I think about how good he's been to me. He's been awfully good to me in my life, you know.... I'm one of those kind who's mostly satisfied.... Lots of folks wouldn't care much for what I think. Lots of folks would think I'm kind of old-fashioned. But I don't care. I'd rather have Jesus. He's all the world to me.** Schmidt affirms, and truly, that Mabel had power—the kind of power Paul prayed that the Ephesians might have, power "to grasp how wide and long and high and deep is the love of Christ" (Eph 3:18). I cite Mabel, equally truly I think, as an example of fortitude—courage with endurance. Power and fortitude are two main ingredients in authentic Christian holiness. "No pain, no gain," but through pain, great gain.

My second example is Terry Waite, the British hostage released at the end of 1991 after nearly five years of solitary con-

---

*Thomas Schmidt, *Trying to Be Good* (Grand Rapids, Mich.: Zondervan, 1990), 182.

finement in Lebanon, chained to the wall of his room for almost twenty-four hours daily. In an interview he said: "I have been determined in captivity, and still am determined, to convert this experience into something that will be useful and good for other people. I think that's the way to approach suffering. It seems to be that Christianity doesn't in any way lessen suffering. What it does is enable you to take it, to face it, to work through it, and eventually to convert it."* Here, too, is a clear testimony to that gain through pain that belongs to authentic holiness.

This is a soft age in the West, an age in which ease and comfort are seen by the world as life's supreme values. Affluence and medical resources have brought secular people to the point of feeling they have a right to a long life, and a right to be free of poverty and pain for the whole of that life. Many even cherish a grudge against God and society if these hopes do not materialize. Nothing, however, as we now see, could be further from the true, tough, hard-gaining holiness that expresses true Christianity.

Rediscovering Holiness, pp. 266–71

---

* *Church Times,* December 27, 1991, 2.

I asked the Lord that I might grow
In faith, and love, and every grace,
Might more of his salvation know
And seek more earnestly his face.

'Twas he who taught me thus to pray,
And he, I trust, has answered prayer;
But it has been in such a way
As almost drove me to despair.

I hoped that in some favored hour
At once he'd answer my request,
And by his love's constraining power
Subdue my sins, and give me rest.

Instead of this, he made me feel
The hidden evil of my heart,
And let the angry powers of hell
Assault my soul in every part.

Yea, more, with his own hand he seemed
Intent to aggravate my woe,
Crossed all the fair designs I schemed,
Blasted my guards, and laid me low.

"Lord, why is this?" I trembling cried,
"Wilt thou pursue thy worm to death?"
"'Tis in this way," the Lord replied,
"I answer prayer for grace and faith.

"These inward trials I employ
From self and pride to set thee free,
And break thy schemes of earthly joy,
That thou mayest seek thy all in me."

ॐ

JOHN NEWTON

Pure Joy

⩫

22

You Are Made for Joy

The word "joy" connects to the desire of our heart. We want joy. We were made for joy. The value of human beings is sometimes affirmed by quoting, from a black source, the words "God don't make no junk." In similar fashion, we may affirm the true goal of human life by saying, "God don't make nobody for misery." If we are miserable, it is because we have chosen to say no to joy. The fact remains that God intended joy for us from the start.

Let me spell that out. Scripture shows that God creates human beings with their joy in view. "Man's chief end is to glorify God, and [in so doing] to enjoy him for ever" (Westminster Shorter Catechism, answer to question 1). Joy was God's plan for man from the beginning. God's purpose that we should enjoy him, both directly in face-to-face fellowship and indirectly through enjoyment of what he has created, is pictured by the fact that the earthly home that he gave Adam and Eve was a pleasure-garden (Eden) where he himself walked in the cool of the day. The psalmist regains a spiritual sanity he had almost lost when he declares: "I am always with you; you hold me by my right hand. You guide me with your counsel, and afterward you will take me into glory. Whom have I in heaven but you? And earth has nothing I desire besides you.... God is the strength of my heart and my portion forever.... It is good to be near God" (Ps 73:23-26, 28). The thought is the same as in Psalm 43:4, where God is called "my joy and my delight." The New Testament tells us that our redemption and life in Christ reverses our damnation and death in Adam (see Rom 5:12-19; 1 Cor 15:21ff.), that God "richly provides us with everything for our enjoyment" (1 Tm 6:17), and that glorified saints endlessly delight in the God whom they endlessly adore (see Rv 7:9-17; 21:1-4; 22:1-5). Thus it appears that God's saving activity vindicates, restores, and fulfills his original purpose of joy for man that satanic malice and human sin have thwarted. Joy to the world remains God's goal.

The New Testament takes us a step further in understanding this. In John's Gospel the veil is lifted on the mutual love and honor that bind Father, Son, and Holy Spirit together in the unity of the one eternal God (see Jn 2:16ff.; 4:34; 5:19-30; 6:38-40; 12:27ff.; 13:31ff.; 14:31; 16:13-15), and Jesus prays to his Father that his disciples may be "one ... in us ... as we are one: I in them and you in me" (Jn 17:21-22). He states his wish "that they may have the full measure of my joy within them" (v.13). God's original purpose was that human beings should share the joyful togetherness of the Trinity, and the gospel of Christ, which proclaims deliverance from sin and is backed up by God's providential kindness (see Acts 14:17; Rom 2:4), is an invitation to enter this joy through penitent and trustful worship. It is in love to the Father and the Son, love that mirrors the Son's love for the Father, that the fullness of joy will be finally found. But sin—self-worship, transgression, unbelief, impenitence—separates us from the joy of God and exposes us to a godless eternity instead (see Jn 3:16-21; Rom 1:18–2:16; Rv 22:11-15). Yet the gospel invitation still stands, and if by embracing sin we miss joy, both present and future, the fault is ours.

Joy is at the heart of satisfied living. It is also at the heart of real and credible Christianity, the Christianity that glorifies God and shakes the world. As joy is, to quote C.S. Lewis, "the serious business of heaven," so it is central to serious godliness on earth. "The kingdom of God is not a matter of eating and drinking, but of righteousness, peace and joy in the Holy Spirit" (Rom 14:17). A joyless Christianity (and joylessness cannot be hidden) will become an obstacle to believing Paul's statement and will render the faith repulsive rather than attractive, whereas a joyful Christianity is a most arresting advertisement for the transforming power of the gospel. So all who do hope to cut ice as witnesses for Christ will do well to study the art of joy as part of their preparation.

Do I arouse eagerness in your heart? Or do I irritate you? There are people who resent the suggestion that joy is for everyone. "Oh," they say, "that may be all right for you, but it's no use for me; it's just mockery as far as I'm concerned." They say that because they are hurting emotionally. If you are hurting, it is hard to believe that there is any possibility of joy for you. You feel bitter and angry when you know that others experience joy and want to pass it on to you. But to readers enmeshed amid the four black *Ds*—disappointment, desolation, depression, desperation—or bogged down in any one of the four black *Fs*—frustration, failure, fear, fury—I wish to say two things.

First, Christians are not victims and prisoners of either the past or the present. The powers of forgiveness and new creation are at work in their lives. Before them lies a sure and certain hope of deliverance, transformation, and glory. Joy will someday be theirs in fullest measure, and they should not give way to the black feeling that life will never be better for them than it is now.

Second, Christians have, so to speak, larger souls than other people; for grief and joy, like desolation and hope, or pain and peace, can coexist in their lives in a way that non-Christians know nothing about. Grief, desolation, and pain are feelings triggered by present situations, but faith produces joy, hope, and peace at all times. This does not mean that grief, desolation, and pain cease to be felt (that idea is inhuman); it means that something else is experienced alongside the hurt. It becomes possible for Christians today, like Paul long ago, to be "sorrowful, yet always rejoicing" (2 Cor 6:10). People who sorrow should be told that God offers them joy whatever their circumstances, for this assurance is just as true for them as it is for anyone else.

Hot Tub Religion, pp. 138–44

My God, the spring of all my joys,
The life of my delights,
The glory of my brightest days,
And comfort of my nights.

In darkest shades, if he appear,
My dawning is begun;
He is my soul's bright morning star,
And he my rising sun.

The opening heavens around me shine
With beams of sacred bliss,
While Jesus shows his heart is mine,
And whispers I am his.

My soul would leave this heavy clay
At that transporting word,
Run up with joy the shining way
To see and praise my Lord.

Long as I live I'll bless thy name,
My King, my God of love;
My work and joy shall be the same
In the bright world above.

ISAAC WATTS

23

What Joy Is Not

Joy is not the same thing as fun and games. Many people "have fun," as we say, seeking and finding pleasure, without finding joy. You can "enjoy yourself" and remain joyless. The restless, relentless pursuit of pleasure (sex, drugs, drink, gadgets, entertainment, travel) is very much a mark of our time, at least in the affluent West, and it clearly indicates a lack of joy. Christians who know the joy of the Lord find that a great deal of fun comes with it, but joy is one thing and fun is another. By contrast, Paul in prison had no fun (that seems a safe statement), yet he had much joy. You can have joy without fun, just as you can have fun without joy. There is no necessary connection between the two.

Joy is not the same thing as jollity, that is, the cheerful exuberance of the person who is always the life of the party, the one who can be relied on for jokes and general effervescence and of whom people say that there's never a dull moment when he (or she) is around. Some Christians are like that, others are not and never will be, but this is a matter of temperament that has nothing to do with joy. One may have a bouncy temperament and yet miss joy, or one may be a low-key person with a melancholic streak, whom no one would ever call "jolly," and yet have joy in abundance. That is good news, for if joy depended on having a jolly temperament, half my readers, and I with them, would have to conclude ourselves unqualified and debarred from joy forever. But the truth is that however our temperaments differ, the life of "joy in the Lord" is available to us all.

I remember as a young Christian hearing a venerable

pulpiteer insist, with great emphasis, that good Christians have teapot faces rather than coffeepot faces. Standard English teapots are spherical, and the teapot face is round, with a big, broad beam and four-inch smile. Standard English coffeepots, by contrast, are long and thin, and the coffeepot face is the same and looks grave and somber. Much impressed by this, I was considerably depressed when next I looked in the mirror! But I reflected that what the preacher had been talking about was bone structure, and bone structure will not be changed till God gives us our new bodies, and so, willy-nilly, my coffeepot face would be mine for life. Did that mean that I could not experience or express Christian joy? Not at all! The preacher's point, that every Christian should radiate joy, was right, but he had made it in the wrong way. The point is that though some people will never be jolly and whoop it up in the way that other people do, both the exuberant ones and the quiet ones may know the joy that is the gift of God.

Joy is not the same thing as being carefree. Advertisements that picture nubile young adults sprawling all over the Bahamas seek to persuade us that "getting away from it all" on vacation is the recipe for joy. Many people agree. But if that is so, as soon as the vacation ends and you return to the responsibilities, burdens, and abrasivenesses of life—the depressing workplace, the uncongenial company, the repeated disappointments—joy will end because you are no longer carefree. Joy, in this view, will only be available to us for our two- or three-week vacation each year! This is the escapist idea of joy; we should be thankful that it is not true.

On the evening of his betrayal and arrest, perhaps twelve hours before his crucifixion, Jesus, who had already indicated that he knew what was facing him, said to his disciples: "I have told you this [i.e., that obedience will keep you in my love] so that my joy may be in you and that your joy may be complete"

(Jn 15:11). These words tell us that joy was his at that moment, though he was not carefree. Similarly, Paul, in prison, living with the possibility of summary execution, was not carefree, yet he had joy in abundance, as the letter to the Philippians vividly shows. Joy despite killing pressure was reality for Jesus and Paul. It has been reality for tens of thousands of Christians since, and it can be reality for us also.

What is joy? We have seen what it is not. A positive definition is now overdue. We focus first on joy in its generic form. Here is my definition: Joy is a happiness of the heart, linked with good feelings of one sort or another. The word "joy" covers the entire spectrum of what may be called the rapturous, ranging from the extreme aching of ecstasy to the quiet thrill of contentment. Webster defines joy thus: "Excitement of pleasurable feeling caused by the acquisition or expectation of good; ... delight; exultation; exhilaration of spirits." Joy is a condition that is experienced, but it is more than a feeling; it is, primarily, a state of mind. Joy, we might say, is a state of the whole man in which thought and feeling combine to produce total euphoria. The preciousness of joy, the integral place of joy in the ideal life, and the pitifulness of joylessness, are apparent from the definition. What, then, is Christian joy? It is, quite simply, basking in the sunshine of the love of our Lord and Savior, Jesus Christ.

Hot Tub Religion, pp. 149–53

꒰

Loved with everlasting love,
Led by grace that love to know;
Gracious Spirit from above,
Thou hast taught me it is so!
O, this full and perfect peace!
O, this transport all divine!
In a love which cannot cease,
I am his, and he is mine.

His forever, only his;
Who the Lord and me shall part?
Ah, with what a rest of bliss
Christ can fill the loving heart!
Heav'n and earth may fade and flee,
First-born light in gloom decline;
But while God and I shall be,
I am his, and he is mine.

꒰

GEORGE W. ROBINSON

24

Joy and Pleasure

[handwritten margin note: False belief ... sadness ... leads to self indulgence ... joy]

Unbelief makes us fear that God is a hard and unfriendly taskmaster who will begrudge us pleasure and require us to do things that we do not want to do and cannot enjoy. Scripture, however, shows us that the opposite is true. "I will be glad and rejoice in you" (Ps 9:2). "You will fill me with joy in your presence, with eternal pleasures at your right hand" (Ps 16:11). "You give them drink from your river of delights" (Ps 36:8). "God, my joy and my delight" (Ps 43:4). "The kingdom of God is ... righteousness, peace and joy in the Holy Spirit" (Rom 14:17). "May the God of hope fill you with all joy and peace as you trust in him" (Rom 15:13).

Christianity, which some believe breeds gloom, actually drives it out. Sin brings sorrow, but piety produces pleasure.

It is sad to find that neither the *Evangelical Dictionary of Theology* (1984) nor any other dictionary of theology known to me has any entry under "pleasure." To be sure, their articles on joy sometimes make shrewd reference to pleasure; look at this, for instance, from *EDT*:

> *Joy.* A delight in life that runs *deeper than pain or pleasure* ... not limited by nor tied solely to external circumstances ... a gift of God ... a quality of life and not simply a fleeting emotion.... The fullness of joy comes when there is a deep sense of the presence of God in one's life.... Jesus made it clear that joy is inseparably connected to love and to obedience (Jn 15:9-14).... There can also be joy in suffering or in weakness when suffering is seen as having a redemptive purpose and

weakness as bringing one to total dependency upon God (Mt 5:12; 2 Cor 12:9).*

That joy is deeper than and not dependent on pleasure is the first thing that needs to be said. Until this has been established, discussion about pleasure in the Christian life is premature. But once it is established that joy does not depend on pleasure, then a positive theology of pleasure becomes possible. And such a theology is needed if we are going to speak to a generation who has learned from Freud (not to mention personal self-knowledge) that the "pleasure principle" is one of the strongest motives in life.

How would a theology of pleasure be formulated? It would have in it at least these points:

Pleasure is (I quote Webster's dictionary) "the gratification of the senses or of the mind; agreeable sensations or emotions; the feeling produced by enjoyment or the expectation of good." Pleasure, like joy, is God's gift, but whereas joy is active (one rejoices) pleasure is passive (one is pleased). Pleasures are feelings, either of stimulation or of tensions released and relaxed in the body, or of realization, remembrance, or recognition in the mind.

Pleasure is part of the ideal human condition. Adam's state was all pleasure before he sinned (Eden, God's pleasure-garden, from which Adam was expelled, typifies that), and when our redemption is complete, pleasure, total and constant, will have become our state forever. "Never again will they hunger; never again will they thirst" (see Rv 7:16ff.). As God made us for pleasure, so he redeems us for pleasure—ours, as well as his. C.S. Lewis' senior tempter Screwtape complains of God, justly from his own point of view, as follows:

---

* Walter A. Elwell, ed., *Evangelical Dictionary of Theology* (Grand Rapids, Mich.: Baker, 1984), 588, emphasis added.

He's a hedonist at heart. All those fasts and vigils and stakes and crosses are only a facade. Or only like foam on the seashore. Out at sea, out in his sea, there is pleasure, and more pleasure. He makes no secret of it; at his right hand are "pleasures for evermore." Ugh!*

Pleasure (conscious enjoyment) has no intrinsic moral quality. What makes pleasures right, good, and valuable or wrong, bad, and sinful is what goes with them. Look at the motivation and outcome of your pleasures. How hard do you chase after them? What kind of behavior do they produce? What is your response to them when they come? If pleasure comes unsought, or as our grateful acceptance of a gift providentially set before us, and if the pleasure does no damage to ourselves or others, and if the delight of it prompts fresh thanksgiving to God, then it is holy. But if the taking of one's pleasure is a gesture of self-indulgence, pleasing oneself with no concern as to whether one pleases God, then, whether or not the action itself is wasteful or harmful, one has been entrapped by what the Bible sees as the pleasures of the world and of sin (see Lk 8:14; Heb 11:25; cf. Is 58:13; 1 Tm 5:6; 2 Tm 3:4; Ti 3:3; Jas 4:3; 5:5; 2 Pt 2:13). The same pleasant experience—eating, drinking, making love, playing games, listening to music, or whatever—will be good or bad, holy or unholy, depending on how it is handled.

Contrast

In the order of creation, pleasures are meant to serve as pointers to God. Pleasure seeking, as such, sooner or later brings boredom and disgust (see Eccl 2:1-11). Yet we have it on the same authority that "a man can do nothing better than to eat and drink and find satisfaction in his work. This too, I see, is from the hand of God, for without him, who can eat or find enjoyment?" (v.24-25.) So "I commend the enjoyment of life" (Eccl 8:15; cf. 9:9). A Jewish rabbi suggested that on Judgment

---

*C.S. Lewis, *The Screwtape Letters* (London: Geoffrey Bles, 1942), 112.

Day God would take account of us for neglecting pleasures that he provided. Christian teachers have rightly insisted that contempt for pleasure, so far from arguing superior spirituality, is actually the heresy of Manichaeism and the sin of pride. Pleasure is divinely designed to raise our sense of God's goodness, deepen our gratitude to him, and strengthen our hope of richer pleasures to come in the next world. That austere Anglo-Catholic moralist C.S. Lewis declares that in heaven the highest raptures of earthly lovers will be as milk and water compared with the delights of knowing God. All pleasures are sanctified and, in fact, increased when received and responded to in this way.

Hot Tub Religion, pp. 64–71

ى

Come, we that love the Lord,
And let our joys be known;
Join in a song with sweet accord,
And thus surround the throne.

The sorrows of the mind
Be banished from the place!
Religion never was designed
To make our pleasures less.

Let those refuse to sing
Who never knew our God,
But children of the heavenly King
May speak their joys abroad.

The God that rules on high,
And thunders when he please,
That rides upon the stormy sky
And manages the seas—

This awful [awesome] God is ours,
Our Father and our love;
He shall send down his heavenly powers
To carry us above.

There we shall see his face,
And never, never sin;
There from the rivers of his grace
Drink endless pleasures in.

So let our songs abound,
And every eye be dry!
We're marching through Emmanuel's ground
To fairer worlds on high.

ॐ

ISAAC WATTS

25

Four Sources of Joy

The knowledge of one's saving relationship to Christ can bring unquenchable joy into believing hearts, and this is something that only Christians can ever understand. "Rejoice in the Lord" means rejoice in being Christ's, in having Christ's Father as your Father, in being right with God the Father and an heir of his glory through Christ's mediation, and in possessing salvation and eternal life as Christ's gift. We are to let joy flow from this source. How will that happen? Through the fulfilling of a four-source formula.

The first source of joy is the awareness that one is loved. *l* Christians know themselves loved in a way that no one else does, for they know that God the Father so loved them as to give his only Son to die on the cross in shame and agony so that they might have eternal life. Every Christian should follow Paul in drawing out the personal implication—"the Son of God ... loved me and gave himself for me" (Gal 2:20).

> *Amazing Love! How can it be*
> *That thou, my God, should'st die for me?*

The measure of love, human and divine, is how much it gives, and by this standard the love of God is immeasurable because both the greatness of the gift and the cost of giving it are beyond our power to grasp. All human parallels fall short; all comparisons are inadequate.

Humbled and awed, Christians should bask daily in the awareness of God's overwhelming, incomparable love.

The second source of joy is the acceptance of one's situation *2* as good. Christians can do this everywhere and always because they know that circumstances and experiences, pleasant and unpleasant alike, are planned out for them by their loving heavenly Father as part of their preparation for glory. "We know that in all things God works for the good of those who love him, who have been called according to his purpose" (Rom 8:28). God's *purpose* is that those whom he calls should be remade so that they become like their Savior, the incarnate Son, Jesus Christ. Their *good* is the fulfilling of this divine purpose for them; and God *works* unceasingly in and through everything that happens so that it becomes in one way or another a means of bringing them closer to the goal.

3   Joy's third source is possession of something worth possessing. Here, too, the Christian is supremely well placed, as we see from Paul's further words about himself. In Philippians 3 we find him celebrating the incomparable worth of the saving relationship with Christ that he now possesses—or, rather, that now possesses him: "I consider everything a loss compared to the surpassing greatness of knowing Christ Jesus my Lord, for whose sake I have lost all things" (v.8). (So he had; he was an up-and-coming rabbi, a top-class Pharisee, a man marked out for distinction as a leader in Judaism. When he became a Christian, he forfeited his status and all his prospects of advancement and found himself having to cope constantly with Jewish plots against his liberty and his life.) "I consider them [i.e., all the things I have lost] rubbish [literally, dung, worthless stuff that can be jettisoned very cheerfully], that I may gain Christ and be found in him, not having a righteousness of my own that comes from the law, but that which is through faith in Christ—the righteousness that comes from God and is by faith" (vv.8-9).

To paraphrase Paul: "I have lost a great deal, but I have gained more. What I have gained is something supremely worth having, something that is glorious and that will grow, broaden, deepen, and become richer to all eternity, namely, an ongoing love relationship with Jesus Christ the Savior. The more I have of it, the more I want of it; thus it establishes itself as the biggest and most valued thing in my life." This is Paul's emphasis, and his words will find an echo in every healthy Christian heart.

Gratitude for this amazing grace prompts the Christian to say, with Paul: "I have Christ. I know Christ. I love Christ. He is the pearl of great price. He is all I want. I am the happiest of human beings, for I am his and he is mine forever, and I will cheerfully let anything go in order to hold on to him and enjoy the full fruits of his love." These thoughts are a third source of joy.

The fourth source of joy is to give something worth giving. This also is an element of Christian experience in a special and unique way. Christ sends believers into the world to be his witnesses, and when they share their knowledge of Christ with others, they know they are giving them the one thing that is supremely worth giving and is, in addition, desperately needed. Paul found joy in the privilege of being put in trust with the gospel, and so should Christians today, even when for the moment the Good News is unappreciated and those to whom one is trying to bring it become rude and offensive in their manner of rejecting it.

As was said earlier, Christians can experience both joy and sadness at the same time. There is joy in making known the Word of Life, even when sorrow is also being felt because the gift has been spurned. But what joy there is when someone to whom one has witnessed comes to faith in Christ.

Christians sometimes find themselves wondering whether their lives are worthwhile, whether they are doing anything that is worth doing. They are sometimes concerned about frittering away precious time and opportunities, wondering whether the serious concerns of adult existence in Christ's service have not slipped through their fingers. Sometimes these feelings are justified; Christians sometimes really are wasting their lives, and there is no joy in that. But Christians who invest time, effort, ingenuity, initiative, and prayer in spreading the gospel and helping build the faith of others do not feel this kind of self-doubt. They have no reason to do so. In a dying world, surrounded by fascinating fellow mortals who because of their sins face a lost eternity, nothing is so well worth doing as sharing the Good News about Jesus and the salvation he gives.

Hot Tub Religion, pp. 155–63

Jesus, I am resting, resting
In the joy of what thou art;
I am finding out the greatness
Of thy loving heart.

Thou hast bid me gaze upon thee,
And thy beauty fills my soul,
For by thy transforming power,
Thou hast made me whole.

Ever lift thy face upon me
As I work and wait for thee;
Resting 'neath thy smile, Lord Jesus,
Earth's dark shadows flee.

JEAN S. PIGOTT

26

Choosing Joy

Paul not only testifies to joy in his own prison experience but commands his Philippian friends to practice joy as a constant discipline of life. "Rejoice in the Lord always," he writes, and repeats himself for emphasis.

Joy is, in fact, one aspect of the fruit of the Spirit, and the habit of rejoicing in the Lord, as the appointed means whereby joy becomes a reality, is as much a matter of divine command and Christian duty as is the doing of any other things. It is true that joy, both natural and spiritual, will periodically come upon us as a gust or glow of unsought exhilaration, an unexpected kiss from heaven as it were, for which we should be grateful every time; but we are not on that account to think of joy as essentially a mood of euphoria for which we ask and then sit down to wait. Joy is habit of the heart, induced and sustained as an abiding quality of one's life through the discipline of rejoicing. Joy is not an accident of temperament or an unpredictable providence; joy is a matter of choice. Paul is directing his readers to choose to rejoice because it is in and through the activity of rejoicing that joy becomes a personal reality.

Paul prays for the Philippians "with joy" because of their partnership in the gospel (see Phil 1:5) and calls them his "joy" (4:1), as he does the Thessalonians, too (see 1 Thes 2:19-20; 3:9). What he means is that when he thinks about them, dwelling on God's grace in their lives, joy flows into his heart. Paul can choose to rejoice in one aspect of a situation of which other aspects are calculated to depress. He rejoices that Christ is being preached and refuses to brood on the bad motives of the preachers or to indulge in self-pity because he is not able to do what they are doing (see 1 Thes 1:15-18). This, more than anything else, makes it clear that joy is a choice; one chooses to focus one's mind on facts that call forth joy. Such is the secret of "rejoicing in the Lord always," namely, to choose what you think about. It is as simple—and as difficult!—as that.

Can we really choose what we are going to think about? In these days, when we are endlessly overstimulated from outside, and the ever-present TV encourages the passive mindset that makes us wait to be entertained, the idea of regularly choosing themes for our thoughts seems strange to the point of freakiness. But Paul has no doubt that thought control of this kind is possible. He actually commands it. "Finally, brethren, whatever is true, whatever is honorable, whatever is just, whatever is pure, whatever is lovely, whatever is gracious, if there is any excellence, if there is anything worthy of praise, think about these things" (Phil 4:8, RSV). Controlling and directing one's thoughts is a habit, and the more one practices it, the better one becomes at it.

Motivation, of course, helps, and Christians have a strong motivation—a deep-rooted urge, instinctive to them as regenerate persons—to center their thoughts on God's grace and glory at all times. As a person in love thinks loving thoughts of the beloved one spontaneously and constantly, so does the regenerate Christian think loving thoughts of God the Savior. It has always been common for Christians to let their thoughts be drawn up to God, magnet as he is to the regenerate mind, and to meditate—that is, talk to themselves and to God, silently or aloud, concerning God's nature, works, and ways, in a manner that prompts praise and adoration and brings endless delight to the heart. Paul's instruction in what to think about simply gives focus and direction to this regenerate instinct, so as to ensure that our meditation will profit us as much as possible.

But what, in particular, are the true, honorable, just, pure, lovely, gracious, excellent, and praiseworthy things on which we are to center our thoughts? They are the doings of God and the fruit of those doings in human lives. They certainly include the fourfold awareness that we have discussed: First, that God loves us, infinitely and eternally; second, that everything comes to us from God, at least with his permission and always under his protection, to further our eternal good; third, that our saving knowledge of the Lord Jesus, which will eternally increase, is something supremely worth having; fourth, that the gospel message of salvation that we seek to pass on to others is something supremely worth giving. These thoughts will always prime the pump of joy in our hearts and thus produce a steady flow of joy, peace (see Phil 4:7, 9), and delight. Try it and see!

Hot Tub Religion, pp. 164–67

Rejoice, the Lord is King!

Your Lord and King adore!

Rejoice, give thanks, and sing

And triumph evermore:

Lift up your heart,

Lift up your voice!

Rejoice, again I say rejoice!

CHARLES WESLEY

27

Joy Here and Hereafter

"Do not love the world or anything in the world. If anyone loves the world, the love of the Father is not in him. For everything in the world—the cravings of sinful man, the lust of his eyes and the boasting of what he has and does—comes not from the Father but from the world. The world and its desires pass away, but the man who does the will of God lives forever" (1 Jn 2:15-17). Love of the world, John the apostle says, in effect, is the root cause of all failures among professed Christians to love God; so whatever you do, do not love the world!

What does it mean to love the world? John analyzes this love in terms of the lust (desire) that says, "I want ..." and the pride (vainglory) that says, "I have...." He is speaking here of restless craving for what you do not have along with complacent crowing about what you do have (v.16). I agree with the NIV's interpretation, quoted above, of John's terse "lust of the flesh, lust of the eyes, and pride of life." The New English Bible renders the last phrase "the glamour of [the world's] life," but that strains the Greek. Passion to possess and pride in possessing what the world around us has to offer is what love of the world means.

From this we see why love of the world excludes love of the Father (v.15). Love of the world is egocentric, acquisitive, arrogant, ambitious, and absorbing, and leaves no place for any other kind of affection. Those who love the world serve and worship themselves every moment. It is their full-time job. And from this we see that anyone whose hopes are focused on gaining material pleasure, profit, and privilege is booked for a bereavement experience, since, as John says (v.17), the world will not last. Life's surest certainty is that one day we will leave worldly pleasure, profit, and privilege behind. The only uncertainty is whether these things will leave us before our time comes to leave them. God's true servants, however, do not face such bereavement. Their love and desire center on the Father and the Son in a fellowship that already exists (cf. 1 Jn 1:3) and that nothing can ever disrupt.

By this analysis John diagnoses for us a moral disease. The essence of the disease is misdirected love and hope, the syndrome of looking exclusively to the existing order of things for present and future delight. To desire and hope is natural to us all, but the snare is to center our highest valuations and expectations on people, things, and events in this world. John indicates the cure—redirection of love and hope, so that for joy and contentment here and hereafter one looks to God alone.

Hot Tub Religion, pp. 83–91

꒰

My thoughts surmount these lower skies,
And look within the veil;
There springs of endless pleasure rise,
The waters never fail.

There I behold, with sweet delight,
The blessed Three in One;
And strong affections fix my sight
On God's incarnate Son.

Light are the pains that nature brings;
How short our sorrows are,
When with eternal future things
The present we compare!

꒰

ISAAC WATTS

28

Live for Heaven

Life should be viewed and lived in terms of two worlds, not just one. Until recently this was a common Christian perspective. Every believer knew it was true and sought to act on it. That fact, quaint though it sounds to modern ears, should cause no surprises. The New Testament is clearly and consistently two-worldly in its teaching. Jesus constantly taught about heaven and hell as the destinies between which men and women choose in this life by the commitments they make, or fail to make.

The joyful hope of either being with Christ upon leaving this world or of seeing him return to welcome his people into a renewed order of things pervades the entire apostolic witness. Basic to New Testament ethics is the belief that Christians should live on earth in the light of heaven, should make decisions in the present with their eye on the future, and should avoid behaving here in a way that would jeopardize their hope of glory hereafter. "Store up for yourselves treasures in heaven, where moth and rust do not destroy, and where thieves do not break in and steal," says Jesus (Mt 6:20). "A man reaps what he sows," says Paul. "The one who sows to please his sinful nature, from that nature will reap destruction; the one who sows to please the Spirit, from the Spirit will reap eternal life. Let us not become weary in doing good, for at the proper time we will reap a harvest if we do not give up" (Gal 6:7-9). All the promises that the glorified Christ in his letters to the seven churches holds out to those who "overcome" the world, the flesh, and the devil, relate to a future state (see Rv 2:7, 10ff., 17, 26-29;

3:5, 12, 21). The many passages of this kind in the New Testament make it obvious that one should live in such a way that the ledgers of eternity will declare one rich before God. This is something no old-time Christian would ever doubt.

For today, by and large, Christians no longer live for heaven and therefore no longer understand, let alone practice, detachment from the world. Nowadays, nonconformity to the world is limited to the means that the world adopts to achieve its goals, and rarely touches the goals themselves. Does the world around us seek pleasure, profit, and privilege? So do we. We have no readiness or strength to renounce these objectives, for we have recast Christianity into a mold that stresses happiness above holiness, blessings here above blessedness hereafter, health and wealth as God's best gifts, and death, especially earthly death, not as thankworthy deliverance from the miseries of a sinful world (the view that the old Anglican Prayer Book expressed), but as the supreme disaster and a constant challenge to faith in God's goodness. Is our Christianity now out of shape? Yes it is, and the basic reason is that we have lost the New Testament's two-world perspective that views the next life as more important than this one and understands life here as essentially preparation and training for life hereafter. And we shall continue out of shape till this proper otherworldliness is recovered. Such otherworldliness does not in any way imply a low view of the wonder and glory and richness that life in this world can have. What otherworldliness implies is that you live your life here, long or short as it may be, seeing everything from the pilgrim perspective immortalized in Bunyan's classic work and making your decisions in terms of your knowledge of being a traveler on his way home.

Peter's first letter spells this out. By God's mercy and through Christ's resurrection, says Peter, believers have a sure hope of glory, for the enjoyment of which God is currently preserving and preparing them (see 1 Pt 1:3-9). So "set your hope fully on the grace to be given you when Jesus Christ is revealed" (v.13), "live your lives as strangers here in reverent fear" (v.17), and "as aliens and strangers in the world, abstain from sinful desires, which war against your soul" (2:11). Endure hostility, human and satanic, without flinching, standing firm in your hope of glory, your loyalty to Christ, and your trust in God the Father, "and the God of all grace, who called you to his eternal glory in Christ ... will himself restore you and make you strong, firm and steadfast" (5:10). That was, is, and always will be the true Christian path.

Hot Tub Religion, pp. 83–91

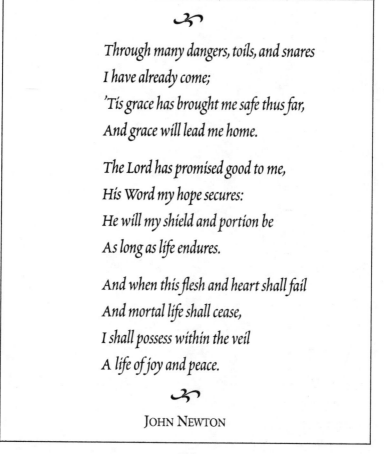

Through many dangers, toils, and snares
I have already come;
'Tis grace has brought me safe thus far,
And grace will lead me home.

The Lord has promised good to me,
His Word my hope secures:
He will my shield and portion be
As long as life endures.

And when this flesh and heart shall fail
And mortal life shall cease,
I shall possess within the veil
A life of joy and peace.

JOHN NEWTON

29

The Thrill of Your Life

In the New Testament we see God's redeeming love and the Christian's hope of glory decisively controlling believers' lives. Paul is a case in point. Paul was so forceful, passionate, and exuberant in his evangelism and pastoral care that the Corinthians thought he was unbalanced—in a word, crazy—and they ridiculed him for it. Paul was not fazed by this. "If we are out of our mind," he retorted, "it is for the sake of God; if we are in our right mind, it is for you." Then he explained why he behaved the way he did. "For Christ's love compels us ..." (2 Cor 5:13-14). *Compels* ("constrains," "overmasters," "leaves us no choice" in other versions) is a Greek word meaning "put under strong pressure." What Paul means is that his knowledge of Christ's atoning love on the cross had enormous motivating force for him, just as it did for the pioneer missionary C.T. Studd, who declared: "If Jesus Christ be God and died for me, then no sacrifice is too great for me to make for him."

It is plain that Paul could have said, with Bunyan's Mr. Standfast, "The thoughts of what I am going to, and of the Conduct that waits for me on the other side, doth lie as a glowing Coal at my Heart." It was God's love and promise that changed Paul's life and made him the man he was.

About this change John also speaks in categorical and universal terms. "This is love: not that we loved God, but that he loved us and sent his Son as an atoning sacrifice for our sins.... We know and rely on the love God has for us.... We love because he first loved us" (1 Jn 4:10, 16, 19). Furthermore: "How great is the love the Father has lavished on us, that we should be called children of God! And that is what we are!...

What we will be has not yet been made known. But we know that when he appears, we shall be like him, for we shall see him as he is. Everyone who has this hope in him purifies himself, just as he is pure" (1 Jn 3:1-3). A person whom hope did not motivate in this way and love did not control would have been diagnosed by the apostle John as not really a believer at all.

The apostolic experience and expectation was that the love and hope Godward that the gospel message evokes would radically transform one's life, both behaviorally, in one's lifestyle, and motivationally, in one's heart. God's love would evoke self-sacrificing love for the Lord and for others. God's promise of heaven would trigger resolution in the face of hostility and discouragement. Resistance to sin—that is, to tempting prospects of pleasure, profit, and privilege in this world—would be strengthened. But did apostles, or anyone else, ever expect this twin evangelical motivation to transform our lives without being turned over and over in the heart by constant meditation? What Paul and John assumed, both from their own experience and from their God-taught understanding of divine grace, was that the reality of redeeming love and the certainty of heaven would so thrill believers' hearts that they would think about these things all the time, just as newlyweds think joyfully and often about the sweetness of their spouses and the delights of all their future plans. And that is how it ought to be!

Hot Tub Religion, pp. 92–95

꙳

One day when heaven was filled with his praises,
One day when sin was as black as could be,
Jesus came forth to be born of a virgin,
Dwelt among men—my example is he!

Living—he loved me, dying—he saved me,
Buried—he carried my sins far away;
Rising—he justified freely, forever:
One day he's coming—O glorious day!

One day the trumpet will sound for his coming,
One day the skies with his glory will shine;
Wonderful day, my beloved ones bringing!
Glorious Savior, this Jesus is mine!

꙳

J. WILBUR CHAPMAN

30

A Glorious New Body

Alone among the world's faiths and "isms" Christianity views death as conquered. For Christian faith is hope resting on fact—namely, the fact that Jesus rose bodily from the grave and now lives eternally in heaven. The hope is that when Jesus comes back—the day when history stops and this world ends—he will "change our lowly body to be like his glorious body" (Phil 3:21; cf. 1 Jn 3:2). This hope embraces all who have died in Christ as well as Christians alive at his appearing. And the raising of the *body* means the restoring of the *person*—not just part of me, but all of me—to active, creative, undying life, for God and with God.

In raising believers, God completes their redemption by the gift, not of their old bodies somehow patched up, but of new bodies fit for new men and women. Through regeneration and sanctification God has already renewed us inwardly; now we receive bodies to match. The new body is linked with the old, yet different from it, just as plants are linked with, yet different from, the seeds from which they grew (see 1 Cor 15:35-44). My present body—"brother ass," as Francis of Assisi would have me call it—is like a student's old jalopy; care for it as I will, it goes precariously and never very well, and often lets me and my Master down (very frustrating!). But my new body will feel and behave like a Rolls-Royce, and then my service will no longer be spoiled.

No doubt, like me, you both love your body because it is part of you and get mad at the way it limits you. So we should. And it is good to know that God's aim in giving us second-rate physical frames here is to prepare us for managing better bodies hereafter. As C.S. Lewis says somewhere, they give you unimpressive horses to learn to ride on, and only when you are ready for it are you allowed an animal that will gallop and jump.

A dwarf I knew would weep for joy at the thought of the body God had in store for him on resurrection day, and when I think of other Christians known to me who in one way or another are physical wrecks—deformed, decaying, crippled, hormonally unbalanced, or otherwise handicapped—I can weep too for this particular element of joy that will be theirs—and yours—and mine when that day dawns.

Very common for three centuries after Christ, and not unknown today was the idea that man's hope is immortality for his soul, which (so it was thought) would be much better if disembodied. There was a tag, "the body is a tomb," which summed up this view. But it shows a wrong view both of matter (which God made, and likes, and declares good) and of man (who is not a noble soul able to excuse the shameful things he does by blaming them on his uncouth material shell, but a psycho-physical unit whose moral state is directly expressed by his physical behavior). The disordering effect of sin is very clear in the way my physical appetites function; but for all that these appetites are part of me and I must acknowledge moral responsibility for whatever active expression they find. The Bible doctrine of judgment is that each of us receives "good or evil, according to what he has done in the body" (2 Cor 5:10).

The promise that one day we shall have bodies "like his glorious body" (Phil 3:21) challenges us—do we really, from our hearts, welcome and embrace our promised destiny of being like Christ? (cf. 1 Jn 3:2ff.) Facing this question could be a moment of truth for us. For some find their whole identity in gratifying physical itches (for sexual excitement, sleep, food, exercise, violence, alcoholic or drug-induced "highs," or whatever) and feel—alas, with too much truth—that were they deprived of these, nothing would be left of them but an ache;

and they see Jesus, who was not led by physical itches, as the "pale Galilean" through whose breath, according to Swinburne, the world grew cold, and whom D.H. Lawrence wanted to humanize (I have to use that verb in fairness to Lawrence, though it is the wackiest nonsense I have ever written) by imagining for him a sex life with a pagan princess. Such a vision makes the idea of being like Jesus—that, and no more—sound like being sentenced to a living death. Now is that how, deep down, it sounds to you?

If so, only one thing can be said. Ask God to show you how Jesus' life, body and soul, was the only fully human life that has ever been lived, and keep looking at Jesus, as you meet him in the Gospels, till you can see it. Then the prospect of being like him—that, and no less—will seem to you the noblest and most magnificent destiny possible, and by embracing it you will become a true disciple. But until you see it—please believe me: I kid you not—there is no hope for you at all.

"Resurrection of the Body," *Growing in Christ*, pp. 83–86

꒰ꕤ꒱

All the way my Savior leads me;
Oh, the fullness of his love!
Perfect rest to me is promised
In my Father's house above:
When my spirit, cloth'd immortal,
Wings its flight to realms of day,
This my song through endless ages:
Jesus led me all the way.

꒰ꕤ꒱

FANNY J. CROSBY

31

Endless Joy

Skeptics like Fred Hoyle and Bertrand Russell have told us that the thought of an endless future life horrifies them; for (they said) it would be so boring! Evidently they have found this life boring, and cannot imagine how human existence could be made permanently interesting and worthwhile. Poor fellows! Here we see the blighting effects of godlessness, and the black pessimism to which it leads.

But not all moderns are like Hoyle and Russell. Some are anxious to survive death. Hence their interest in spiritist phenomena, supposed to give proof of survival. But three facts should be noted. First, "messages" from the departed are distressingly trivial and self-absorbed. Second, "messages" do not come from those who in this life walked close to God. Third, mediums and their "controls" are embarrassed by the name of Jesus. These facts give warning that the spiritist phenomena, whatever their true explanation, are a blind alley for investigating "the blessed hope of everlasting life."

Everlasting life does not just mean endless existence but the final joy into which Jesus entered (see Heb 12:2), and which he promised and prayed that his followers would one day share. "Where I am, there shall my servant be also; if any one serves me, the Father will honor him." "Father, I desire that they also, whom thou hast given me, may be with me where I am, to behold my glory" (Jn 12:26; 17:24).

Being with Jesus is the essence of heaven; it is what the life everlasting is all about. "I have formerly lived by hearsay and faith," said Bunyan's Mr. Standfast, "but now I go where I shall live by sight, and shall be with him, in whose company I delight myself." What shall we do in heaven? Not lounge around!—but worship, work, think, and communicate, enjoying activity, beauty, people, and God. First and foremost, however, we shall see and love Jesus, our Savior, Master, and Friend.

The everlastingness of this life was spelled out in the vividest possible way by the anonymous benefactor who appended to John Newton's "Amazing Grace" this extra verse:

When we've been there ten thousand years,
Bright shining as the sun,
We've no less days to sing God's praise
Than when we first begun.

I have been writing with enthusiasm, for this everlasting life is something to which I look forward. Why? Not because I am out of love with life here—just the reverse! My life is full of joy, but my reach exceeds my grasp. My relationships with God and others are never as rich and full as I want them to be, and I am always finding more than I thought was there in great music, great verse, great books, great lives, and the great kaleidoscope of the natural order.

As I get older, I find that I appreciate God, and people, and good and lovely and noble things, more and more intensely; so it is pure delight to think that this enjoyment will continue and increase in some form (what form, God knows, and I am content to wait and see), literally forever. Christians inherit in fact the destiny that fairy tales envisage in fancy: *we* (yes, you and I, the silly saved sinners) *live*, and live *happily*, and by God's endless mercy will live happily *ever after*.

We cannot visualize heaven's life, and the wise man will not try. Instead, he will dwell on the doctrine of heaven, which is that there the redeemed find all their heart's desire: joy with their Lord, joy with his people, and joy in the ending of all frustration and distress and the supply of all wants. What was said to the child—"If you want sweets and hamsters in heaven, they'll be there"—was not an evasion, but a witness to the truth that in heaven no felt needs or longings go unsatisfied. What our wants will actually be, however, we hardly know, save that first and foremost we shall want to be "always ... with the Lord" (1 Thes 4:17, RSV).

Often now we say in moments of great enjoyment, "I don't want this ever to stop"—but it does. Heaven, however, is different. May heaven's joy be yours, and mine.

"The Life Everlasting," *Growing in Christ*, pp. 87–89

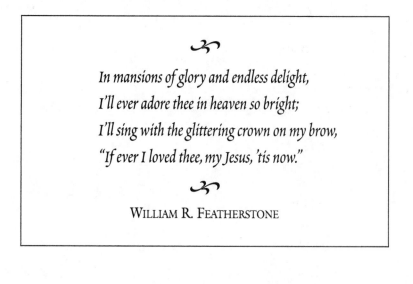

In mansions of glory and endless delight,
I'll ever adore thee in heaven so bright;
I'll sing with the glittering crown on my brow,
"If ever I loved thee, my Jesus, 'tis now."

WILLIAM R. FEATHERSTONE

Bibliography

Hot Tub Religion. Wheaton, Ill.: Tyndale House, Living Books, 1987.

God's Words. Grand Rapids, Mich.: Baker, 1988.

Gott Lieben Und Seine Gebote Halten. Geissen: Brunnen Verlag, 1991.

Growing in Christ. Wheaton, Ill.: Good News/Crossway, 1994.

Rediscovering Holiness, Ann Arbor, Mich.: Servant, 1992.

Tenth, a periodical formerly published by Tenth Presbyterian Church, Philadelphia, Pennsylvania.